Student Activity Workbook

COMPANION TO

Ruby

Mosdos Press
Cleveland, Ohio

acknowledgments

ISBN # 0-9801670-3-5 Student Activity Workbook
COPYRIGHT © 2009
MOSDOS OHR HATORAH, CLEVELAND, OHIO
All rights reserved. Printed in the U.S.A.

This publication is protected by copyright and all duplication or reproduction is prohibited. Storage in a retrieval system, or transmission in any form or by any means, electronic, mechanical, photocopying, recording, or otherwise are also prohibited. This copyright will be strictly enforced. For information contact Mosdos Press, 1508 Warrensville Center Road, Cleveland Heights, Ohio 44121.

EDITOR-IN-CHIEF
Judith Factor

DESIGN/COMPOSITION DIRECTOR
Carla Martin

SENIOR EDITOR
Abigail Rozen

COPY EDITOR
Laya Dewick

INSTRUCTIONAL TEXT WRITERS
Abigail Rozen, Rifky Amsel

TEXT AND CURRICULUM ADVISOR
Rabbi Ahron Dovid Goldberg

table of contents

UNIT ONE

The Things That Matter

Leah's Pony 2
Supergrandpa 8
Two Big Bears 14
Mom's Best Friend 20
The Tiger, the Persimmon and the Rabbit's Tail 24

UNIT TWO

Clarity

Sato and the Elephants 28
Amelia's Road 36
The Hatmaker's Sign 40
Dad, Jackie, and Me 46
And Now the Good News 50

UNIT THREE

Head, Hands, Heart

Eddie, Incorporated 56
Heatwave! 62
The Wright Brothers 68
The Imperfect/Perfect Book Report 72
Justin Lebo 78

table of contents

UNIT FOUR

Caring

Earthquake Terror 84
The Gift 92
Toto 98
Owl Moon 104
Homeward the Arrow's Flight 108

UNIT FIVE

Determination

Underwater Rescue 116
The Seven Children 124
The Garden of Happiness 128
One Grain of Rice 132
Maria's House 136

UNIT SIX

The Grand Finalé

The Bridge Dancers 140
Dancing Bees 146
Name This American 150
Boss of the Plains 158
Stone Fox 164

Mosdos Press

Educators transmitting appropriate values and academic excellence

Leah's Pony

VOCABULARY
Activity 1

| agriculture | clutched | cultivate | drought | sow |
| auctioneer | collateral | debt | gullies | withered |

1. Abe's parents owned an antique shop. He and his sister, Jean, would often make up stories about the buyers and sellers who came into the shop. If an old woman came into the shop, a bag _____ (held onto tightly) in her hand, Jean would say something like, "I bet she was born a princess, and is selling the last of her jewels because she has become so poor."

2. If a young man came in to sell something, Abe would say, "Oh! I'll bet he's gotten himself into _____ (something that is owed) by borrowing money to pay for that motorcycle parked outside."

3. Part of owning an antique shop involved going to auctions to buy antiques to sell in the store. Abe and Jean loved hearing the _____ (the person who conducts the auction) auction off the pieces for sale.

4. Often, there would be other auctions held right in the same place. One week, the auction included many tools and vehicles used in _____ (farming).

5. Some tools were to be used for harvesting; others were used to _____ (help the plants grow) the ground and ready it for planting.

6. All sorts of interesting characters turned out for the farm auctions. One week, a farmer brought a big, fat _____ (an adult, female pig) to auction off.

7. The other farmers laughed. "What kind of tool is that?" hollered one. "It ain't a tool," he hollered back. "It's _____ (property promised as guarantee for a loan) that I'm putting up if someone will give me the loan of their tractor."

8. "What happened to your tractor?" bellowed another farmer. "Well," said the farmer, "first we had no rain at all. We had a regular _____ (a long period of dry weather)."

9. "The crops dried up and _____ (shriveled). The ground was as hard as rocks."

10. "Then the rains came. They made all kinds of holes and _____ (small valleys and ravines made by running water) in the ground. My poor old antique tractor just can't handle that kind of job." My parents, hearing the word "antique," bought the old tractor to use as part of a display in front of their store, and a farmer loaned him a tractor. Everyone went home happy.

Unit One: The Things That Matter ~ (Textbook p. 4)

Name _____

Leah's Pony
VOCABULARY
Activity II

Words are tools that we use to express our thoughts. If we organize words into groups the way a worker organizes his tools, we will be able to find them when we need them. In *Leah's Pony*, you learned six words having to do with farming. Put them in the middle drawer of your tool chest. You learned three words connected to money. Put them in the bottom drawer of your tool chest. One last word remains. Put it in the top drawer of your tool chest.

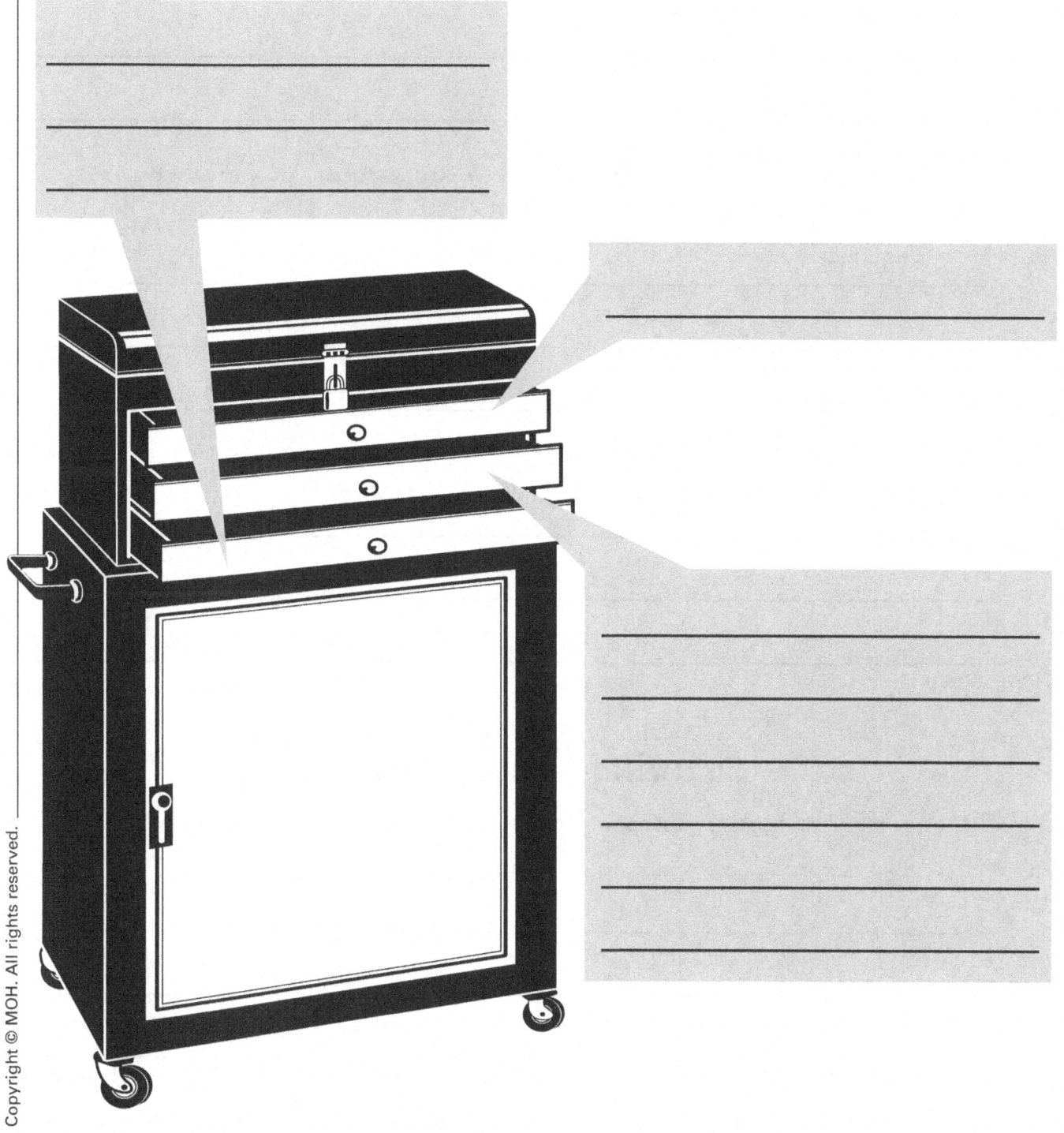

Unit One: The Things That Matter ~ (Textbook p. 4)

Leah's Pony

COMPREHENSION Questions

In-Depth Thinking

1. What was the same and what was different for Leah's family before their land was struck by the drought and after their land became part of the "Dust Bowl"? List two things that remained the same and two things that changed.

   _____
   _____
   _____

2. Many close bonds and friendships appear in this story. Write down examples of at least two of them.

   _____
   _____
   _____
   _____

3. What do you think will happen now that the auction is over?

   _____
   _____
   _____
   _____

Drawing Conclusions

4. Why do you think Leah's parents first spoke in hushed voices but later shared their troubles with her?

   _____
   _____
   _____
   _____

Unit One: The Things That Matter ~ (Textbook p. 4)

Name _____

Leah's Pony

COMPREHENSION

Questions

5. Mama was very resourceful and reused many items in order to save. Can you think of some ways you can reuse items in your daily life to avoid waste?

_____
_____
_____

6. Leah had an idea that turned out to be very helpful to adults. Think of a time when you provided adults with an idea or suggestion. How was the idea received? If you have never had an experience like this, you may make one up.

_____
_____
_____

One Step Further

Parting with precious belongings is not easy for adults or children. Imagine that you had to auction off some of your own possessions to help your family. Write a paragraph that includes the answers to the following questions. What items would you choose and what price would you attach to them? Would you cooperate with the family auction and be proud to contribute or would you be angry and resentful?

_____
_____
_____
_____
_____
_____

Unit One: The Things That Matter ~ (Textbook p. 4)

Leah's Pony

GRAPHIC ORGANIZER
Contrasting

Leah's Pony is about sacrifice. *Sacrifice* means giving up something that is very precious to you, for the sake of someone (or something) else. People make a sacrifice hoping it will make a bad situation better.

In *Leah's Pony*, many people make sacrifices. Fill out the chart below by telling what the person *could* have done if he or she were more selfish. Then, write down what each character actually did.

	What Each Could Have Done	What Each Did
Farmer One		
Farmer Two		
The Neighbors	The neighbors could have bid on the tractor and animals and gotten a real bargain.	They remained silent.
Mr. B.		
Leah		

Whose sacrifice do you think was the greatest? Why do you think so?

_____

_____

_____

Unit One: The Things That Matter ~ (Textbook p. 4)

Leah's Pony

GRAPHIC ORGANIZER — Visual Images

Name _____

Leah's Pony is a tale of hard times and soft hearts. The author helps us to feel the beauty of the countryside and the harshness of the weather by using images. An **image** is a "picture" that a writer "draws" with words. An image helps you to *imagine* what the author is describing.

Here is an example:

"That whole summer, Leah and her pony crossed through *cloud-capped cornfields*."

In the exercise below, answer the question in each picture frame with a phrase from the story. Then, choose one of the phrases and draw a picture of it in the last picture frame. On the line under the frame, write the phrase.

- How did the pony's coat look after it was brushed?
- How tall did the corn grow?
- How hard did the wind blow, some days?
- How did the farm look when the grasshoppers came?
- Leah raced her horse past a deserted house. How did the house look?

Unit One: The Things That Matter ~ (Textbook p. 4)

Supergrandpa

VOCABULARY — Activity 1

| contestants | orb | scoffed | spry | triumph |
| craned | rivalry | sprinted | surpass | vigorous |

1. Grace and Bertha were two lively and _____ (energetic) old ladies who enjoyed taking part in contests and competitions.

2. Although they had gray hair and wrinkled faces now, when they were young, they were _____ (people who take part in a competition) in their town's famous running marathon.

3. They were still good friends, but their _____ (competition) had not disappeared as they got older.

4. So, when the big bake-off was announced, the two old rivals entered, each determined to do as well as, or even _____, (outdo) the other.

5. The audience chuckled as the eight elderly ladies _____ (raced at full speed for a short distance)—well, at least hobbled as fast as they could—to the baking tables.

6. The audience then _____ (stretched out) their necks to watch as the ladies mixed the batter in their bowls.

7. People were surprised to see how strong and _____ (active) each of the ladies looked as they measured, poured, mixed, kneaded, and stirred.

8. Even the teenagers, who had _____ (mocked) at the whole contest, were full of admiration for the bakers.

9. As the big, red _____ (a round object) of the sun began to set, and the deadline approached, the entire audience waited to see who would win the contest.

10. When the judges announced that Grace and Bertha had tied for first place, the two friends cheered and hugged each other, happy in their _____ (victory).

Unit One: The Things That Matter ~ (Textbook p. 24)

Name _____

Supergrandpa

VOCABULARY

Activity 11

Meet Mixed-Up Moby

Moby is a student who sometimes confuses the meanings of words. It is up to you to straighten Moby out!

Mixed-Up Moby thinks that:

1. to **scoff** means to make a mark on your shoe. It doesn't!
   It means to _____

2. to **sprint** is to call someone on your cell phone.
   It's not! It is to _____

3. to **crane** is to drive a machine that is used in building tall buildings.
   It's not! It is to _____

4. an **orb** is a plant used in making teas and medicines.
   It's not! It is _____

5. **spry** describes a detective or an undercover agent.
   It doesn't! It describes _____

6. a **contestant** is a student taking an exam.
   It's not! It's _____

7. to **surpass** is something highway drivers do if the car in front of them is going too slow.
   It's not! It's _____

8. a **triumph** is an instrument that you blow.
   It's not! It is _____

9. **rivalry** means learning how to shoot a rifle. It doesn't!
   It means _____

10. **vigorous** could mean a European wig-wearing walrus (a **vig**-vearing-val**rus**), but even Moby knows that's kind of silly!
    It really means _____

Unit One: The Things That Matter ~ (Textbook p. 24)

Supergrandpa

COMPREHENSION Questions

In-Depth Thinking

1. What was Gustaf's original reason for wanting to ride in the Tour of Sweden bicycle race? What became his new purpose once the race began?

   _____
   _____
   _____

2. Describe the character traits that helped Gustaf participate in and 'win' the race.

   _____
   _____
   _____

3. List three important events in the story in the order in which they happened.

   _____
   _____
   _____

Drawing Conclusions

4. We cannot always judge a person's ability to do something based on age alone. Look at what Gustaf was able to accomplish. Describe someone you know who is old, yet young at heart. Write about how this person was able to accomplish something even though other people thought he or she would not be successful.

   _____
   _____
   _____
   _____

Unit One: The Things That Matter ~ (Textbook p. 24)

Name _____

Supergrandpa
COMPREHENSION
Questions

5. At what point did you realize that Gustaf was capable of winning the race? Use words from the story to help explain your answer.

_____
_____
_____

6. Why do you think Gustaf received so much of the public's attention?

_____
_____
_____

One Step Further

There is a famous saying, "Don't judge a book by its cover." What do you think this means? Do you think it is true? Write a paragraph about a time that you judged something by its 'cover.' An example would be that you thought the new dish your mother was serving for supper looked awful but, after tasting it, you decided it would become one of your all-time favorites.

_____
_____
_____
_____
_____
_____
_____
_____

Unit One: The Things That Matter ~ (Textbook p. 24)

Supergrandpa

GRAPHIC ORGANIZER — Grouping Ideas

Nobody believed in Gustaf—except Gustaf. Once Gustaf refused to be discouraged and entered the race in spite of everything people said, people began to take notice. Soon, they were cheering him on.

Supergrandpa can be divided into three parts. The first part could be called: what people said to discourage Gustaf. The second part could be called: what Gustaf did because he believed in himself. The third part could be called: what people said or did to encourage Gustaf.

"Ride with Supergrandpa" on the "road" below, by answering the questions in each section of the road. When you reach the end, wait! The king is coming to greet you!

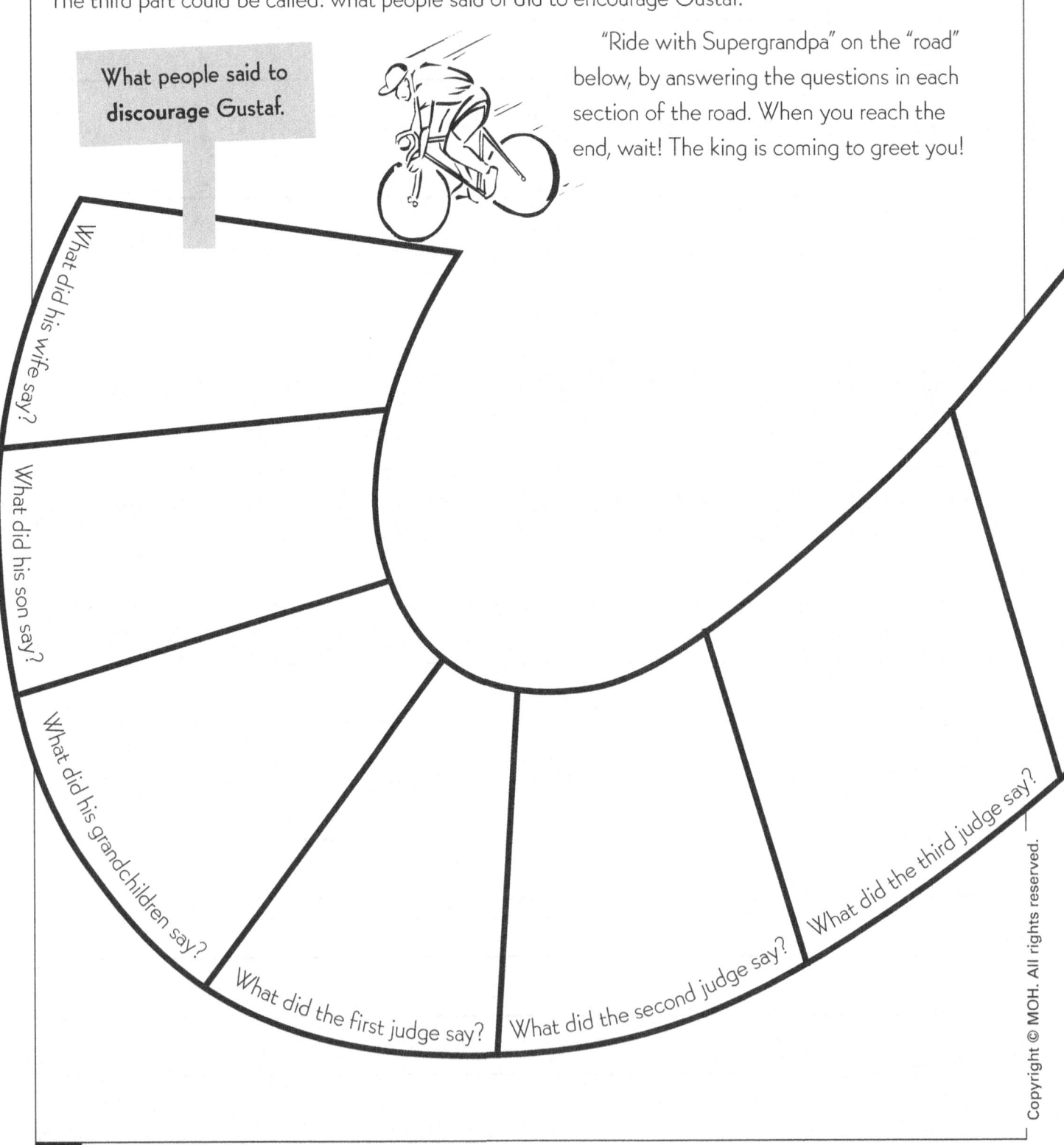

Unit One: The Things That Matter ~ (Textbook p. 24)

Name _____

Supergrandpa

GRAPHIC ORGANIZER

Grouping Ideas

What Gustaf did.

- What did Gustaf do the morning after the judges rejected him?
- What did Gustaf do to reach Haparanda?
- What did Gustaf do because he didn't have a number?
- How did Gustaf get ahead of the other riders?
- What didn't Gustaf do?
- How did the newspaper make him famous?
- How did people help him when he was hungry?
- How did he become known to radio audiences?
- What did they tell him near the end of the race?
- What did they do when he won?

What people said or did to encourage Supergrandpa.

Unit One: The Things That Matter ~ (Textbook p. 24)

Two Big Bears

VOCABULARY
Activity 1

| budge | chores | eaves | pitch | thaw |
| calico | club | hearth | quiver | trembling |

1. It was my old house. I stood in front of it, my heart pounding and my hands _____ (shaking slightly from fear).

2. I was almost as afraid and excited as I had been the day the snows melted, the day we called "the great _____ (melt)."

3. Twenty-five years ago, I had been an ordinary ten-year-old boy, going about the yard, doing my _____ (everyday work; small jobs) so that I would be allowed to play when I was done.

4. My job was to shake the snow off the tree branches and knock it off the roof and the _____ (overhanging lower edges of a roof) of the house.

5. I wasn't quite sure how I was going to knock down the snow. The mild weather had made the snow rock-hard, and no matter how hard I pushed it with my broom and shovel, it wouldn't _____ (move even slightly).

6. Thick, heavy icicles were hanging from the roof. I decided to try to knock those down with a wooden _____ (heavy stick).

7. As I stood near the window, knocking down icicle after icicle, my nose began to twitch and _____ (shake slightly).

8. Smoke! I looked inside and the room, usually so bright and sunny, was as black as _____ (a black, sticky tar).

9. I saw that the red and white _____ (a plain cotton fabric printed on one side) curtains at a different window had caught fire.

10. A log had apparently rolled off the fire, onto the _____ (the floor of a fireplace), and the wind had blown sparks around the room. A moment later, the entire family ran out of the house. We thought the house would burn to the ground, but we were wrong! The fire turned the snow on the roof to water, which poured into the living room and put out the fire. What a day to remember!

Unit One: The Things That Matter ~ (Textbook p. 40)

Name _____

Two Big Bears

VOCABULARY

Activity II

Where Would You Find...?

Circle the correct answer.

1. meat that has thawed
   a. in the freezer
   b. on your kitchen counter
   c. on the dinner table

2. leaves
   a. on trees
   b. on buses
   c. on houses

3. quivering
   a. in angry dogs
   b. in frightened kittens
   c. in strict teachers

4. calico
   a. in a fabric store
   b. in a candy store
   c. in a doctor's office

5. chores
   a. with instructions for a game of checkers
   b. on a to-do list your mother has left you
   c. in Aunt Betty's recipe for apple pie

6. pitch
   a. with other materials used for waterproofing
   b. with other sprays used to kill insects
   c. with other soaps used in houses

6. trembling
   a. in the trunks of tall, sturdy trees
   b. in loud, blasting music
   c. in the voices of nervous, frightened speakers

7. a club
   a. among the fish
   b. in a library
   c. with sticks and branches

8. a hearth
   a. in a hospital
   b. by a fireplace
   c. near the ocean

9. something that will not budge
   a. a swift racehorse
   b. a slow turtle
   c. a stubborn mule

Unit One: The Things That Matter ~ (Textbook p. 40)

Two Big Bears

COMPREHENSION Questions

In-Depth Thinking

1. There are a number of characters in the story (Pa, Ma, Laura, Mary, the shopkeeper, the men in the shop, Sukey, Ma's bear, and Pa's 'bear'). Which ones do you think were very important and necessary to the story and which ones were not so important?

   _____
   _____
   _____
   _____

2. In what way were Sukey and the bear similar? In what way were they different?

   _____
   _____
   _____
   _____

3. Think of two events that could have taken place at the Little House in the Big Woods in the week following the story.

   _____
   _____
   _____

Drawing Conclusions

4. How old do you think Laura was at the time of this story?

   _____
   _____

Unit One: The Things That Matter ~ (Textbook p. 40)

Name _____

Two Big Bears
COMPREHENSION
Questions

5. Ma told the girls that everything was all right. Do you think that she really felt that way?

_____
_____
_____

6. Ma did not show just how frightened she was when she discovered that the glittering eyes belonged to a bear. She did not fight the bear, but hurried to the house. Pa was clearly frightened, yet started to fight the bear (even though it turned out to be a stump). How were the two situations different? Was one parent braver than the other, or were they equally brave?

_____
_____
_____

One Step Further

It is clear from the story that Laura's family is close-knit and that they all care for one another. Describe some of the things that make you feel cared for. Some examples would include: your mother tucking you in at night and checking on you when you're asleep; your grandfather hugging you close and slipping you a dollar every time he visits; or your teacher asking if you're feeling better after you've been absent from school.

_____
_____
_____
_____
_____
_____
_____

Unit One: The Things That Matter ~ (Textbook p. 40)

Two Big Bears

GRAPHIC ORGANIZER

Parallels in a Story

Mirror Image

Two Big Bears is a beautiful story of a young girl growing up on the American frontier. The author makes the story especially interesting by using parallels. That means that the two main characters, Papa and Mama, have experiences that are very similar. For example, Papa's frightening experience with the "bear" is at night. Mama's frightening experience with the "cow" (that is really a bear) takes place at night, too.

In the following exercise, there is one face for Papa's experiences and one for Mama's. We have chosen five parallels from the story, but have given you only one half of each parallel. Choosing from the sentences in the answer box on the next page, write the other half of the parallel on the line provided.

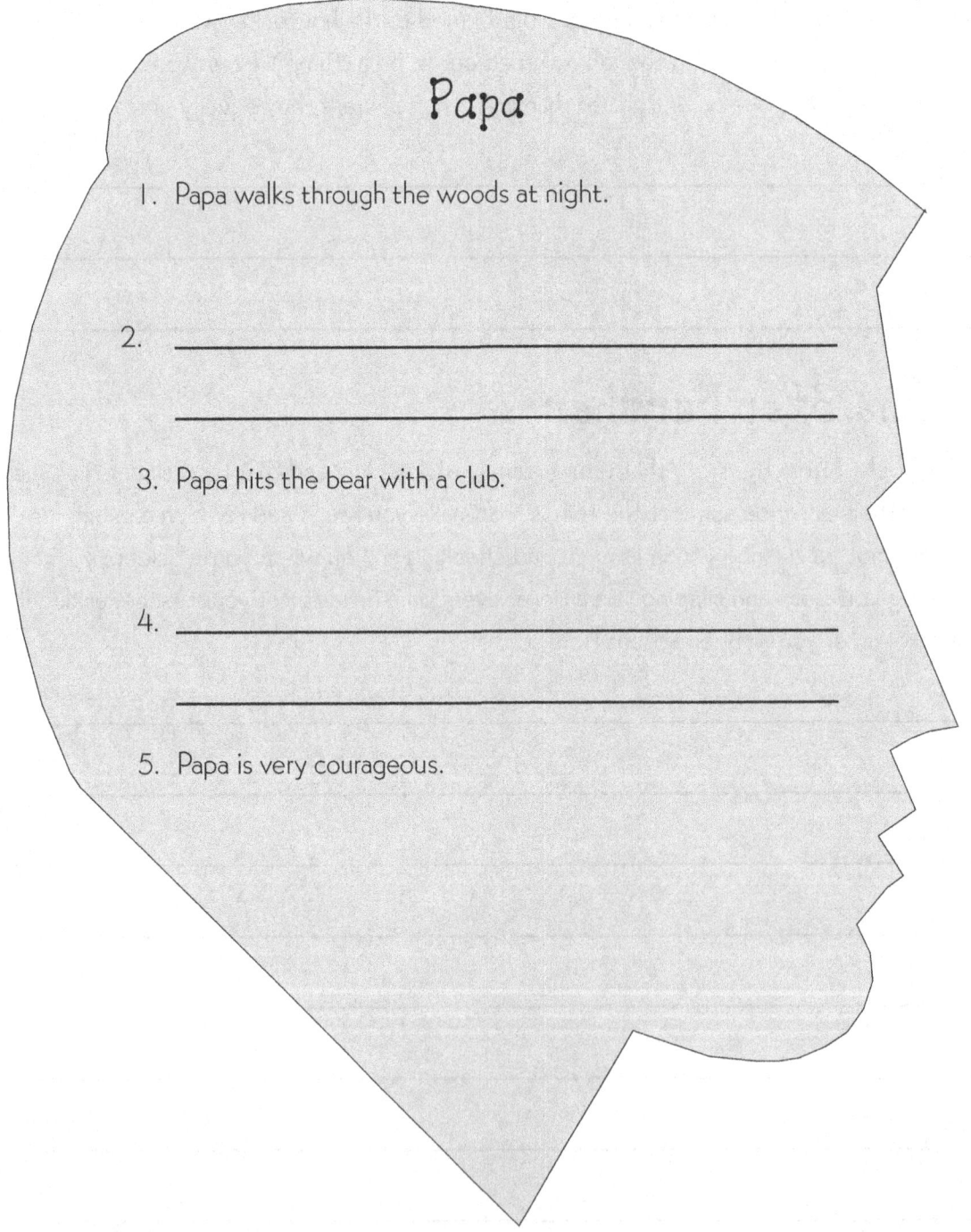

Papa

1. Papa walks through the woods at night.

2. _____
   _____

3. Papa hits the bear with a club.

4. _____
   _____

5. Papa is very courageous.

Unit One: The Things That Matter ~ (Textbook p. 40)

Two Big Bears

GRAPHIC ORGANIZER

Parallels in a Story

Name _____

> Mama hits the "cow."
> Mama is very courageous.
> Mama goes to the barn at night.
> Papa thinks he sees a bear.
> After Papa hits the "bear," he finds it is a tree.

Mama

1. *Mama goes to the barn at night.*

2. Mama thinks she sees a cow.

3. _____

4. After Mama hits the "cow," she realizes it is a bear.

5. _____

Unit One: The Things That Matter ~ (Textbook p. 40)

Mom's Best Friend

COMPREHENSION Questions

In-Depth Thinking

1. Why was the training a vacation for Mom while, for the rest of the family, it felt like something very different?

   _____
   _____
   _____
   _____

2. Think of three other situations that, like garbage day, would be challenging for dog guides.

   _____
   _____
   _____
   _____

3. Explain why patience is a character trait needed by the main characters in the story.

   _____
   _____
   _____
   _____

Drawing Conclusions

4. Have you ever become attached to something or someone and found it hard to "let go" the way Leslie found it hard to let go of Marit?

   _____
   _____
   _____
   _____

Name _____

Mom's Best Friend

COMPREHENSION

Questions

5. Would you react the way Leslie reacted if you were in her position? Would you look at the situation differently? Do you think you would understand Mom's actions better than Leslie did? Explain.

_____

_____

_____

6. After reading about someone who is unable to see, a common reaction is to stop a moment and feel gratitude for all of the amazing functions of the body. Write about a part of your body that you are especially grateful for.

_____

_____

_____

One Step Further

A dog is a man's best friend.

Do you agree or disagree with this statement? Support your answer. Whether you agree or disagree, would your answer change if you were thinking about someone like Leslie's Mom?

_____

_____

_____

_____

_____

_____

_____

Unit One: The Things That Matter ~ (Textbook p. 58)

Mom's Best Friend

GRAPHIC ORGANIZER
Applying Literature to Life

It is amazing that Mom can do so many different things! Although she is blind, she cooks, cleans, jogs, plays the piano, and generally leads a happy, normal life. How does she do it? Think of all the things that can help her. She will use her sense of smell, her hearing, her sense of touch, a dog guide, a cane, another person, and other things not mentioned. In addition, considerate people will remove anything that might hurt her or keep her from moving around freely.

The chart is divided into three columns. The first column lists the things Mom enjoys doing. In the middle column, explain how she can do these things without being able to see. You may look back at the story or use your common sense to find the answers. In the third column, describe how people who can see could help make each of these activities safer and easier for a blind person.

Everyday Activities		
cross the street		
walk along a tree-lined sidewalk		
cook on the stove		
bake in the oven		
ride in an elevator		
jog		
vacuum the carpet		
ice skate		
play the piano		
read a book		
sort the laundry		
shop at the supermarket		

Unit One: The Things That Matter ~ (Textbook p. 58)

Name _____

Mom's Best Friend

GRAPHIC ORGANIZER

Applying Literature to Life

How Mom Does Them	How We Can Help

Unit One: *The Things That Matter* ~ (Textbook p. 58)

The Tiger, the Persimmon and the Rabbit's Tail

COMPREHENSION Questions

In-Depth Thinking

1. The tiger is described as very confident and strong at the beginning of the story. Do you think that the tiger is as confident and strong at the end of the story?

   _____
   _____
   _____

2. What does the tiger say that shows how frightened he is?

   _____
   _____
   _____

3. The tiger is a coward, but he is also a bad "thinker." What mistakes did the tiger make in his reasoning?

   _____
   _____
   _____
   _____

Drawing Conclusions

4. How was the rabbit's reaction to the 'dried persimmon' different from the tiger's? Why was it different?

   _____
   _____
   _____
   _____

Unit One: The Things That Matter ~ (Textbook p. 72)

Name _____

The Tiger, the Persimmon and the Rabbit's Tail

COMPREHENSION

Questions

5. Do you think the thief will steal again in the future? Why or why not?

_____

_____

_____

6. Why did the tiger consider the human baby's crying noisy and annoying? Surely his roar and other sounds in the forest were louder!

_____

_____

_____

One Step Further

What did the other animals think when they heard the story about the huge, roaring tiger? Write a conversation that takes place between some animals in which they talk about the tiger and what happened to him. Your animals may (but don't have to) have different personalities. One may be serious, another may be sarcastic, and a third may be funny.

_____

_____

_____

_____

_____

_____

_____

_____

Unit One: The Things That Matter ~ (Textbook p. 72)

The Tiger, the Persimmon and the Rabbit's Tail

GRAPHIC ORGANIZER
Compare and Contrast

We laugh as we watch the tiger, the thief, and the rabbit doing silly things because they have jumped to the wrong conclusions. The following exercise helps you compare what *really* happened with what each character *thought* was happening. It also helps you remember what ridiculous things each character did because of these many misunderstandings.

Complete the chart by filling in the empty boxes with the description called for at the top of each column.

What Actually Happened
A mother said, "Stop crying! Do you want the tiger to get you?"
The baby kept crying.
The thief felt the tiger's fur.
The thief thinks he should get away as fast as possible.
The tiger feels the thief riding on his back.

Unit One: The Things That Matter ~ (Textbook p. 72)

Name _____

The Tiger, the Persimmon and the Rabbit's Tail
GRAPHIC ORGANIZER
Compare and Contrast

What Mistake Was Made	What Was Done Because of the Mistake
The tiger thought the mother knew he was there.	The tiger crept closer to the house.
The tiger thought a persimmon was scary and strong.	
	He thinks he is going to die.
The tiger thinks the dried persimmon is off his back.	
The rabbit wants to know what a dried persimmon is.	The rabbit hops to the tree and looks for the dried persimmon.
The rabbit thinks the man is harmless.	
	The rabbit runs away minus his tail.

Unit One: The Things That Matter ~ (Textbook p. 72)

Sato and the Elephants

VOCABULARY
Activity 1

| beacon | corroded | eerie | pare | tepid |
| chiseled | dense | flaw | precision | trudged |

1. My friends and I looked at each other through the fog as we floated in our old, rusty, _____ (worn away) boat.

2. The plan had been to sail down the coast and explore the old lighthouse. It was a _____ (a light used as a warning signal) to all the boats in the area.

3. Unfortunately, the plan was a careless one, without _____ (being exact about every detail).

4. No one had considered the weather; this was a major _____ (defect) in the plan.

5. Instead of the sunshine that we expected, a _____ (thick and tightly packed together) fog hung over us.

6. The lighthouse looked dark, spooky, and _____ (strange and somewhat frightening).

7. Not knowing what to do, we decided to wait and see if the fog would lift. Joey offered to core and _____ (to cut off the outer layer) some apples for us to snack on.

8. When he passed around the apples, we saw that he had _____ (carved) the apples so that they looked like little smiling faces.

9. After our snack, we rowed our little boat closer to the lighthouse and decided to wade through the _____ (lukewarm) water to the steps of the lighthouse.

10. As we _____ (walked slowly and heavily) through the water and up to the lighthouse, the sun suddenly broke through the clouds. Perhaps the outing would be a success, after all.

Unit Two: Clarity ~ (Textbook p. 94)

Sato and the Elephants

VOCABULARY

Activity 11

Name _____

Mixed-Up Moby is Back!

Do you remember Mixed-Up Moby? Moby is a likable, very imaginative student who sometimes mistakes one word for another. It is your job to straighten things out!

Mixed-Up Moby thinks that:

1. to **pare** is to match up.
   It's not! It's _____

2. **tepid** is a sort of tent used by American Indians.
   It's not! It's _____

3. **flaws** are something you walk on.
   They're not! They're _____

4. **eerie** is a lake in Ohio.
   It's not! It means _____

5. **trudge** is a really good, chocolatey candy.
   It's not! It means to _____

6. **dense** is something you do at weddings and parties when the music begins.
   It's not! It means _____

7. **precision** is something you make when you have more than one choice. It's not!
   It means _____

8. **beacon** is something some people eat with eggs.
   It's not! It's _____

9. **chiseled** is a way of describing ice cream with chocolate drizzled on it.
   It's not! It means _____

10. **corroded** describes a restaurant that is *crowded* and *loaded* with customers.
    It's not! It means _____

Unit Two: *Clarity* ~ (Textbook p. 94)

Sato and the Elephants

COMPREHENSION Questions

In-Depth Thinking

1. How did Sato decide what to carve out of the piece of ivory?

2. Sato's father was very important to him when he was growing up. How do you know this?

3. Where did the bullet come from?

Drawing Conclusions

4. Why was Sato feeling guilty? What did he do as a result of his guilt?

5. The story begins by telling us that Sato was a happy man. Was he happy at the end of the story as well? Explain.

Name _____

Sato and the Elephants

COMPREHENSION

Questions

6. Are you interested in becoming a master at something? What is the 'something'?

_____
_____
_____

One Step Further

Sato kept the ivory elephant where he could see it day and night. Do people generally like to be reminded of their mistakes? Why or why not? Why do you think Sato displayed the elephant even though it reminded him of his past?

Sato and the Elephants

GRAPHIC ORGANIZER

Tracing Character Development

Have you ever seen the sun come up? At first, the sky is pitch black. Then, the night seems just a little less dark. Little by little, the sky turns from black, to gray, to pale blue, to white and, suddenly, the sun bursts on the scene and the whole world lights up!

Life can be like that, too. We may be completely in the dark about an important idea. That means we know nothing about it. Then, we begin to learn about the idea in bits and pieces. Finally, we really understand it. This new understanding can change our lives.

At the beginning of the story, Sato is young and innocent. He knows that ivory comes from elephants, but he has never thought about how the ivory gets into the hands of people. As the story moves along, Sato has a slow awakening. He begins to realize that something must die for—what? For a beautiful statue!

The questions in the following exercise trace Sato's slow change from a boy who carved ivory to a young man who could not do it anymore. Answer the question in each block in the exercise.

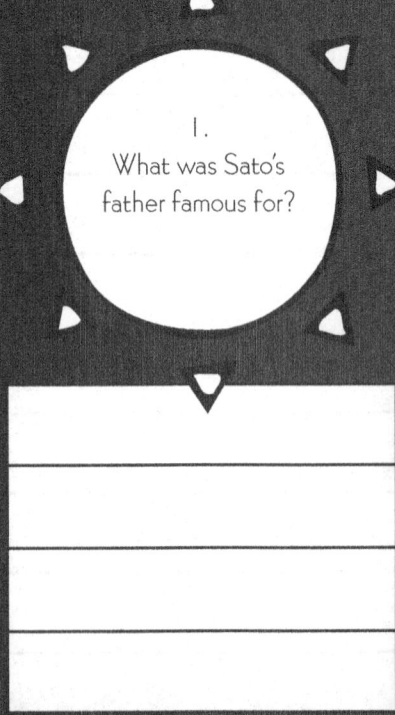

Unit Two: *Clarity* ~ (Textbook p. 94)

Name _____

Sato and the Elephants

GRAPHIC ORGANIZER

Tracing Character Development

3. Where in the story does Sato first think about where ivory comes from?

4. When Sato looks at the beautiful piece of ivory he has bought from Akira, what vision appears to him?

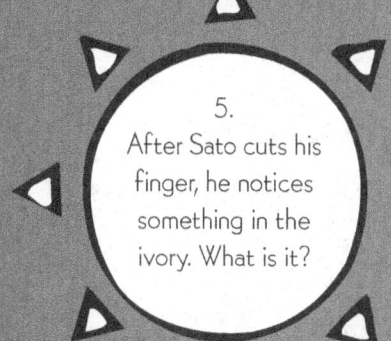

5. After Sato cuts his finger, he notices something in the ivory. What is it?

Unit Two: Clarity ~ (Textbook p. 94)

Sato and the Elephants

GRAPHIC ORGANIZER
Tracing Character Development

6. What does Sato suddenly understand (even though he knew it before)?

7. When Sato understands this, what does he do?

Unit Two: *Clarity* ~ (Textbook p. 94)

Name _____

Sato and the Elephants

GRAPHIC ORGANIZER

Tracing Character Development

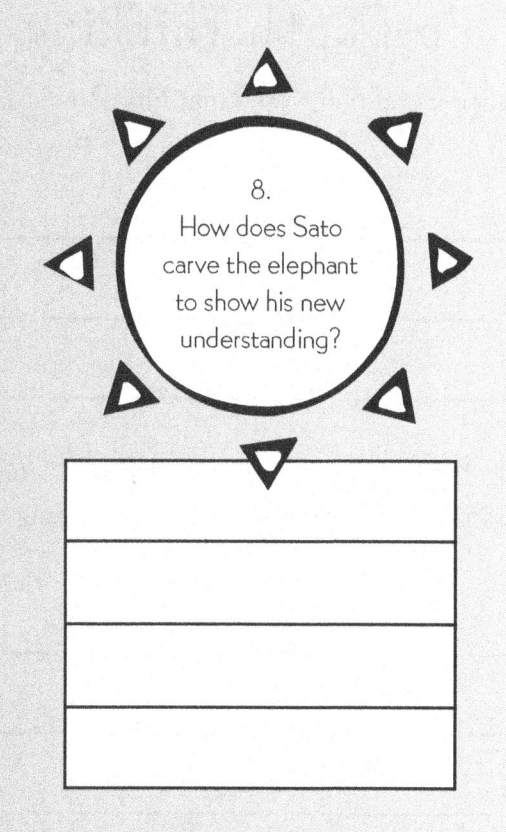

8.
How does Sato carve the elephant to show his new understanding?

9.
In his dream, what does Sato think the elephants will do to him?

10.
How do we know that Sato really feels that elephants should not be killed for their ivory?

Unit Two: *Clarity* ~ (Textbook p. 94) 35

Amelia's Road

COMPREHENSION Questions

In-Depth Thinking

1. Compare Amelia's attitude and mood before she met Mrs. Ramos and found the tree, to those she had afterwards.

2. Some children do not like to be singled out in front of the class, while others like the attention. How did Amelia feel when Mrs. Ramos put a red star on her paper and showed it to the entire class?

3. Why do you think Amelia buried the box instead of taking it with her?

Drawing Conclusions

4. Describe a moment when an experience, smell, or sight caused you to remember another time or place. (For example, fresh-cut grass might remind you of a time when you were in summer camp.) Is there something besides a date that reminds you of a special event?

Name _____

Amelia's Road

COMPREHENSION

Questions

5. How do you think Amelia will hold onto the feeling of belonging when she moves to a new place?

   _____
   _____
   _____

6. Describe an external conflict you once had with a person or a situation.

   _____
   _____
   _____
   _____

One Step Further

While Amelia says that roads never go where one wants them to, in the end she finds a road that she likes. It leads her to a place that she wants to be, a place that gives her a warm sense of belonging and connection. Where would you like a road to take you? What might you find at the end of it that will symbolize finding what you dream of?

_____
_____
_____
_____
_____
_____
_____
_____

Unit Two: *Clarity* ~ (Textbook p. 112)

Amelia's Road

GRAPHIC ORGANIZER
Grouping Ideas

Most of us feel we belong somewhere. We have an address, a phone number, a school we go to, a dentist we visit. These things do not change much. They may remain the same for many years. Amelia's family were migrant workers. They moved from place to place. Almost everything in their life changed all the time. Amelia felt there was no one place she could call home. Then, she found the accidental road and the big tree at the end of it. By burying some items in a box under the tree, she created a place she could come back to and find just the way it was when she left.

Amelia's family did not have a house or apartment. They moved from place to place.

Mrs. Ramos showed Amelia's picture to the class.

Unit Two: Clarity ~ (Textbook p. 112)

Name _____

Amelia's Road

GRAPHIC ORGANIZER

Grouping Ideas

In each of the cars on the opposite page, write one reason Amelia felt she did not belong anywhere.

Now, follow the road across the page. What are three wonderful things that helped Amelia feel she belonged? Write one event in each section of the road.

Find Amelia's box under the tree. Inside the box, draw a picture of something she put into it to make her feel as though she belonged somewhere.

Unit Two: *Clarity* ~ (Textbook p. 112) 39

The Hatmaker's Sign

VOCABULARY
Activity 1

| absurd | cobblestones | haughty | parable | quibbling |
| apprentice | delegate | magistrates | parchment | sympathetic |

1. Nicholas was ten years old. "It is high time," said his father, "that you learn a skill. I have arranged for you to become an _____ (*a person who works for another in order to learn a trade*) to the baker, starting next week."

2. It was the year 1776. The city of Boston was busy. The streets echoed with the sound of horses' hooves pounding on the _____ (*small, rounded stones used in paving roads*).

3. Men hurried to and fro, many of them holding books or scrolls of _____ (*a stiff, heavy paper made from the skin of animals*) in their hands.

4. Some of them held their heads high, looking proud and _____ (*snobbish*).

5. Some of the men walked along deep in conversation, discussing politics or _____ (*arguing over small, unimportant details*) about a new law.

6. Nicholas enjoyed the hustle and bustle of the streets. He especially liked to watch the soldiers walk by. He knew that his father had been _____ (*understanding and supportive*) to the Revolution before and during the war. Now he was thrilled that America had won its independence.

7. The only people Nicholas did not really like were the _____ (*government workers who enforce the law*), who acted as if they were very important.

8. He thought that they looked _____ (*ridiculous*) in their shiny hats and bright uniforms.

9. They reminded him of the peacocks in a _____ (*a short story designed to teach a true or moral lesson*) he had read.

10. Nicholas worked and waited. He did not mind baking, but what interested him most was the new American government. His dream was to be chosen as a _____ (*a person sent by a group to represent them at a meeting or a convention*) to represent Boston in Congress when he grew up.

The Hatmaker's Sign

VOCABULARY

Activity 11

Name _____

When you know a lot of words, you can "shop" in your mind until you find just the right one. Read the shopping list below, and select the jar, can, box, or bottle that contains just the word you need.

Shopping List for words that describe:

1. that snobby Mr. Peters who lives down the street _____

2. young George who is learning to be a silversmith _____

3. what cranky Mrs. Fairfax does about every little detail _____

4. Jean Bolton, our town's representative _____

5. a symbolic story with a message _____

6. Mr. Thorne, who is a type of policeman _____

7. heavy, ivory paper on which to write something very important _____

8. my dog, Jesse, who can always tell when I'm in a bad mood _____

9. the way Mindy looked in that ridiculous hat _____

10. what they used to pave that old-fashioned street, Ivy Lane _____

Cans: absurd | delegate | haughty | parable | quibbling

Bottles: apprentice | cobblestones | magistrates | parchment | sympathetic

Unit Two: Clarity ~ (Textbook p. 130)

The Hatmaker's Sign

COMPREHENSION Questions

In-Depth Thinking

1. What are some similarities and differences between what happened to John and what happened to Thomas Jefferson? List something that was the same and something that was different.

   _____
   _____
   _____

2. What do you think of the comments that were made to John on the way to the sign maker's shop? Choose two of the comments and write what you think of them. You may think a comment was helpful, insulting, funny, and so forth.

   _____
   _____
   _____

3. Do you think that Benjamin Franklin helped Thomas by telling him the story? Write a sentence or two about how you think Thomas reacted to the story.

   _____
   _____
   _____

Drawing Conclusions

4. What type of internal conflict might John have had while listening to all of the comments about his sign? Write a little imaginary conversation John had in his mind as he meets the different characters along the way. For example:

   "Here comes Lady Manderly. Oh, no. She always makes me nervous."

   "John, my boy, you were raised to be polite. Just greet her with a smile."

   "But her advice is always so ridiculous."

   "You have to look like you think it is wise."

Unit Two: *Clarity* ~ (Textbook p. 130)

Name _____

The Hatmaker's Sign

COMPREHENSION

Questions

_____
_____
_____

5. Both Thomas and John thought their creations were perfect. Were they? Answer the question in one or two sentences.

_____
_____
_____

6. John put a few words on the sign for his new shop. The apprentices thought a picture was enough for the sign. Professor Wordsworth thought a sign was not even necessary. What do you think?

_____
_____
_____

One Step Further

A **dialogue** is a conversation between two people. In Ben Franklin's story about the hatmaker, John meets Reverend Brimstone, Lady Manderly, a magistrate, and two young apprentices. They all suggest that his sign needs to be changed. In each case, John tells them they are probably right. Imagine that he had told them they were most definitely wrong! Choose *one* of the four meetings, and write some lines for John to use as a response.

_____
_____
_____
_____

Unit Two: *Clarity* ~ (Textbook p. 130)

The Hatmaker's Sign

GRAPHIC ORGANIZER
Writing Skills

Thomas Jefferson thought carefully about every word of the Declaration of Independence. Have you ever tried to write a perfect letter or composition? It usually looks like this:

Some sentences you write are too long. Some are too short. After a lot of work, you get it just right. Ben Franklin told a story about a sign that was made too short. But some signs are too long. It takes work to get writing just right!

In the following exercise, you are going to work on a sign for three different businesses: an ice cream shop, a pet store, and a dentist's office. You will make three signs for each business. The first one will be too long. The second will be too short. The third will be just right!

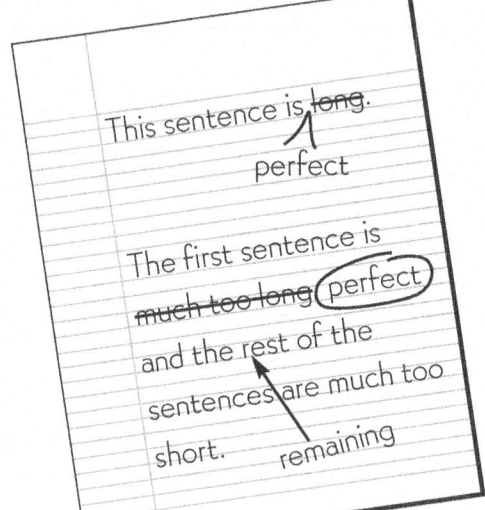

> This sentence is ~~long~~.
> ↑ perfect
>
> The first sentence is ~~much too long~~ (perfect)
> and the rest of the
> sentences are much too
> short. ← remaining

Unit Two: *Clarity* ~ (Textbook p. 130)

Name _____

The Hatmaker's Sign

GRAPHIC ORGANIZER
Writing Skills

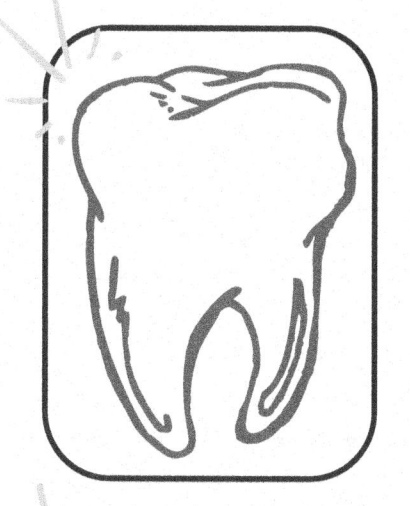

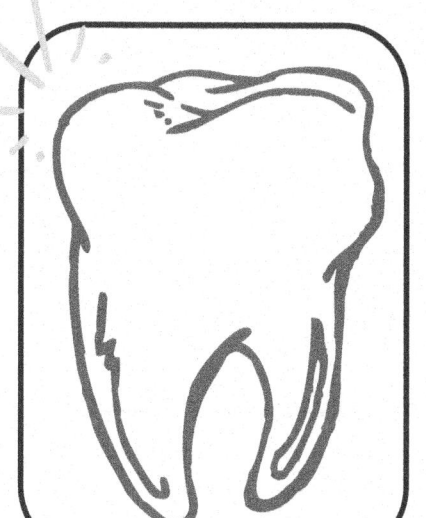

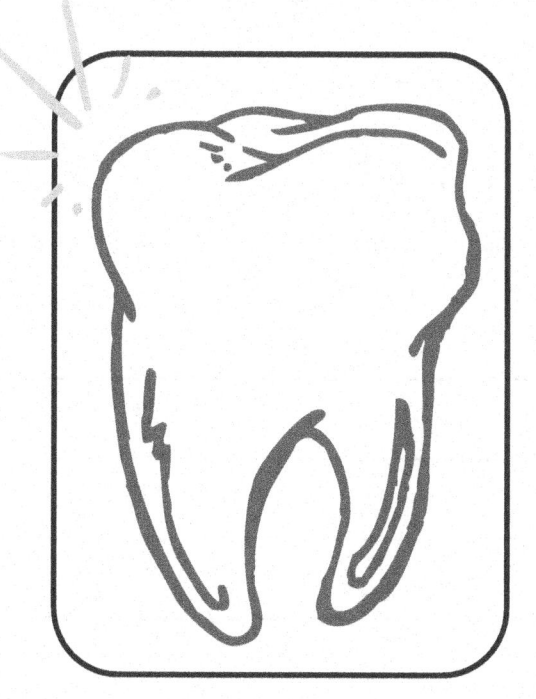

Unit Two: *Clarity* ~ (Textbook p. 130)   45

Dad, Jackie, and Me

COMPREHENSION
Questions

In-Depth Thinking

1. Compare how the author feels about his father at the first baseball game they attend to the way he feels about him at the last game they attend.

   _____
   _____
   _____

2. Why were there stares the first time Dad screamed "Jackie!", but not later on?

   _____
   _____
   _____

3. What are some similarities between Jackie Robinson and Dad?

   _____
   _____
   _____
   _____

Drawing Conclusions

4. Dad kept on learning baseball terms, the details of the game, and how to catch a ball. If he did not enjoy baseball, why did he continue?

   _____
   _____
   _____
   _____

Name _____

Dad, Jackie, and Me
COMPREHENSION
Questions

5. Why do you think that Jackie stood alone at first base staring at his glove after the game was over?

_____
_____
_____

6. How do you think the New York Giants felt when they lost the last game? What about all of the people watching?

_____
_____
_____

One Step Further

Jackie Robinson was the first black baseball player in the major leagues. Many other black baseball players followed. Write an imaginary conversation between Jackie and the next black player to join the Dodgers. What might the new player ask or say to Jackie? What advice might Jackie give him?

_____
_____
_____
_____
_____
_____
_____
_____

Unit Two: *Clarity* ~ (Textbook p. 146)

Dad, Jackie, and Me

GRAPHIC ORGANIZER — Outlining Plot

This story is the story of three different struggles.

It is the struggle of the Brooklyn Dodgers to win the pennant.

It is the struggle of Jackie Robinson to be accepted as a regular member of the team.

It is the struggle of Dad to learn baseball and participate as a fan even though he is deaf.

On these two pages, there are three baseball diamonds, one for each struggle in the story. **First, second, and third base of each baseball diamond represent one step in the plot that brings the team or person closer to victory.** Some of the "bases" have been filled in for you. Fill in the rest of the bases.

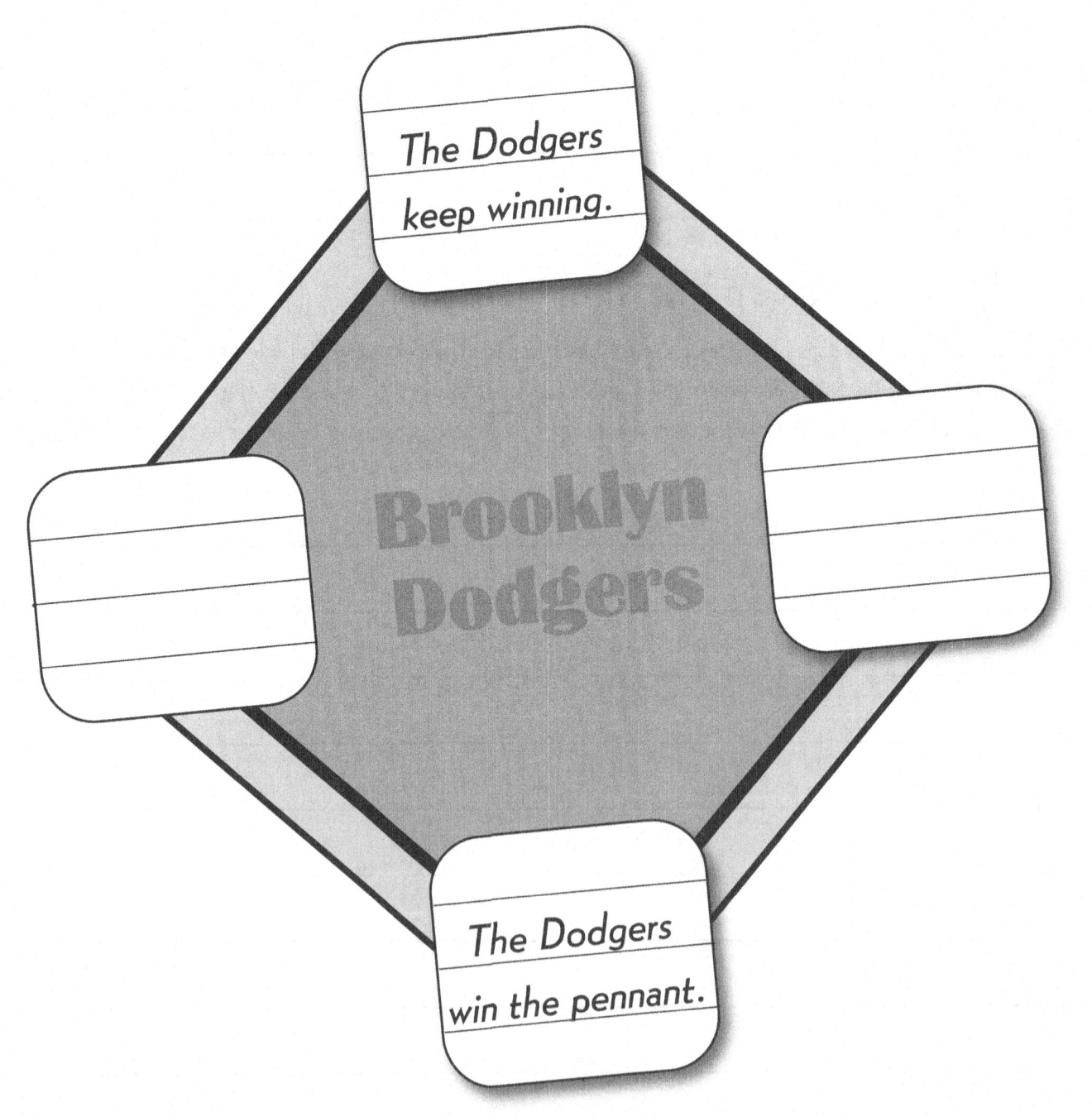

Second base: The Dodgers keep winning.

Third base: _____

First base: _____

Home (center): Brooklyn Dodgers

Home plate: The Dodgers win the pennant.

Unit Two: *Clarity* ~ (Textbook p. 146)

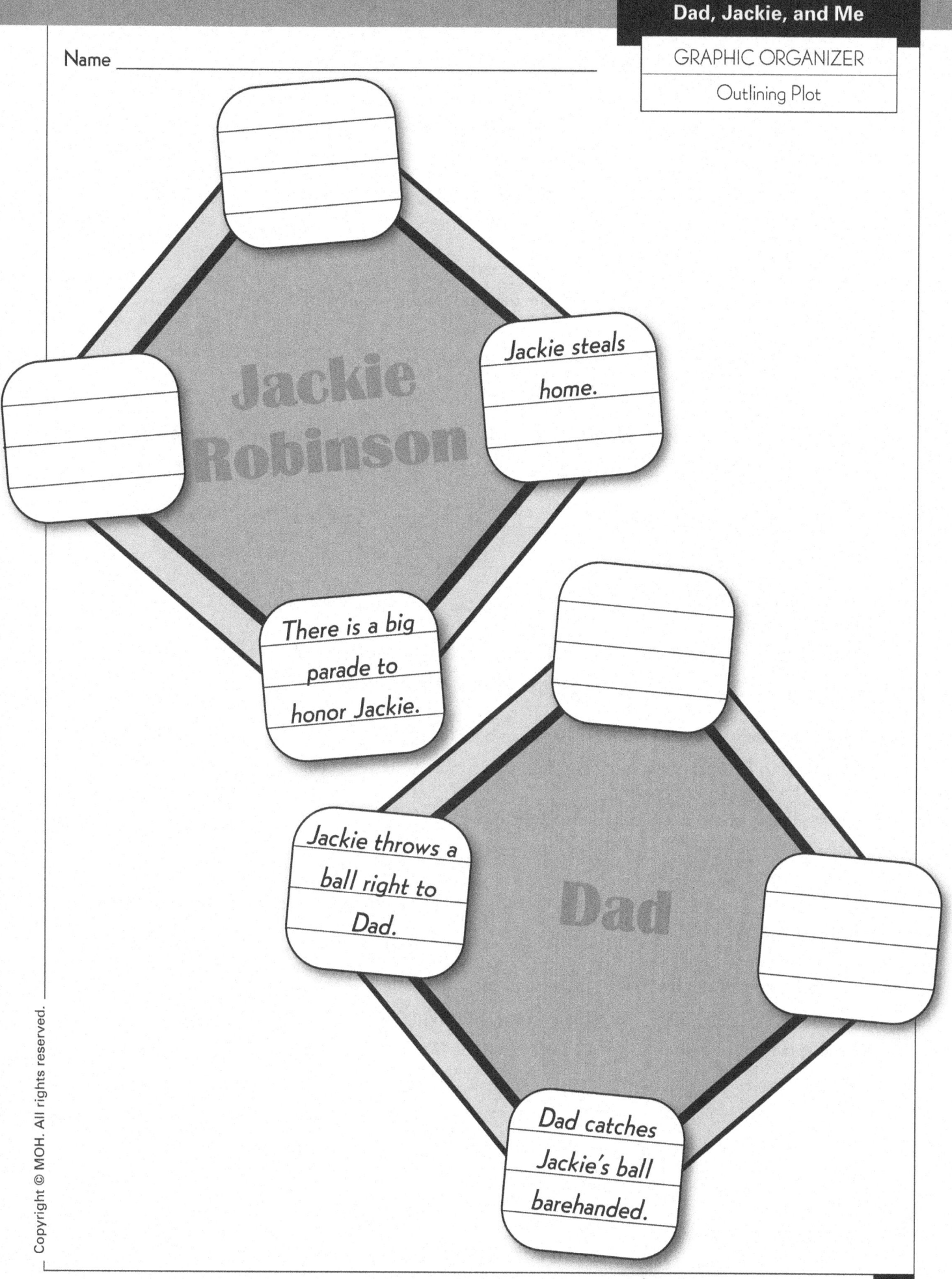

Name _____

Dad, Jackie, and Me

GRAPHIC ORGANIZER

Outlining Plot

Jackie Robinson

- Jackie steals home.
- There is a big parade to honor Jackie.

Dad

- Jackie throws a ball right to Dad.
- Dad catches Jackie's ball barehanded.

Unit Two: Clarity ~ (Textbook p. 146) 49

And Now the Good News

VOCABULARY
Activity 1

| basking | expedition | ornery | rehabilitation | thrives |
| commercial | habitat | predator | sanctuary | transport |

1. My dog is the laziest dog on the face of the earth. He spends most of his day _____ (*lying in something pleasantly warm*) in the sun.

2. He was born thinking his natural _____ (*the place where a plant or animal is naturally found*) is a soft rug in front of the fireplace.

3. If he could talk, he would probably tell you that our home is one of those places where wildlife is protected, a sort of _____ (*land set aside where wildlife can live safely*).

4. This dog does not exercise. He _____ (*grows and improves*) on rest and relaxation.

5. To him, a long, dangerous _____ (*a journey or voyage*) is a trip to the corner.

6. At one time, we tried to teach him to bring my father the newspaper. You would think he was being asked to _____ (*move; carry*) a ton of bricks.

7. He also has expensive taste in food. No store-bought, _____ (*made by companies to be sold; not homemade*) dog food for him!

8. My dog is almost always in a good mood. He is just too lazy to be _____ (*mean*).

9. If any _____ (*an animal that hunts other animals for food*) ever attacked him, he'd be a "goner."

10. He would probably let himself get bitten and then go to the dog hospital for _____ (*a returning to good health*). And that, my friends, is why we love him!

Name _____

And Now the Good News

VOCABULARY

Activity II

Professor Peel has just returned from an expedition. He plans to write a book with nine chapters. Each chapter will be about a different adventure that he had on his journey. It is your job to select a title for each chapter. Look at the two titles suggested for each chapter, and underline the one that best describes what that chapter is about. A hint about each vocabulary word is given in italics. The first one is done for you.

1. In Chapter One, Professor Peel starts his expedition by visiting a *large area in which plants and animals of all kinds can live without being harmed by man*.
   Example: **The Magnificent Sanctuary** • The Green Predator

2. In Chapter Two, the professor writes more about the area, saying how the animals *grow and do really well* in this wonderful place. A Time for Rehabilitation • A Place to Thrive

3. In Chapter Three, Professor Peel continues on his journey where, unfortunately, he meets up with a *mean* and hungry dog. The Basking Collie • The Ornery Terrier

4. In Chapter Four, Professor Peel, who has been scratched and bitten by the dog, must take some time off *to recover* from his injuries. The Professor's Habit • Professor Peel's Rehabilitation

5. In Chapter Five, Professor Peel, almost healed, enjoys *lying* in the sunshine on the beach, getting stronger every day. Basking on the Beach • Expedition in the Sunshine

6. In Chapter Six, Professor Peel, all better, is eager for excitement. He goes in search of *animals who hunt other animals*, so he can photograph them. In Search of Habitats • Where Are the Predators?

7. In Chapter Seven, Professor Peel spends several weeks in a jungle that is the *home* of the animals he is searching for. He finds them. A Month in the Commercial Jungle • Living in an Animal Habitat

8. In Chapter Eight, the professor, loaded down with the many pictures he has taken, plus all of his equipment, hires some natives to *move* his belongings to his next destination.
   Transporting My Possessions • Rehabilitating My Work

9. In Chapter Nine, our professor, happy but weary from his travels, heads for home on a ship loaded with sacks of flour that will be used *in businesses* like bakeries and factories. Unfortunately, he is allergic to wheat, so he spends most of the journey sneezing. Gezundheit!
   Transporting Goods for the Homemaker • Sailing on a Commercial Ship

Unit Two: *Clarity* ~ (Textbook p. 162)

And Now the Good News

COMPREHENSION Questions

In-Depth Thinking

1. How have zoos changed over the years?

   _____
   _____
   _____

2. Write two things about alligators that changed after a law was passed to protect them.

   _____
   _____
   _____

3. What types of animals are often captured illegally? What do people use them for?

   _____
   _____
   _____

Drawing Conclusions

4. What problems occur when animals raised in captivity are placed back into the wild?

   _____
   _____
   _____

5. How can preserving and protecting animal habitats help humans?

   _____
   _____
   _____

Name _____

And Now the Good News

COMPREHENSION

Questions

6. What are some things the author tells us that people can do to help the environment? List a few things you can do personally to help the environment.

_____
_____
_____
_____

One Step Further

Make up a story about a group of friends who make a great effort to help the environment. Describe how they are successful and influence all the people who learn about their project.

_____
_____
_____
_____
_____
_____
_____
_____
_____
_____
_____

Unit Two: *Clarity* ~ (Textbook p. 162)

And Now the Good News

GRAPHIC ORGANIZER
Organizing Facts

The author of *And Now the Good News* writes, "When a large predator like the alligator thrives, dozens of smaller animals thrive with it… Protecting a large animal is a real bargain because it saves whole ecosystems."

When the three diagrams are filled out, they illustrate the "bargain" we get when a large animal is protected. In the small circles around the alligator and the elephant, write the names of some of the smaller animals who "thrive" with it.

54   Unit Two: *Clarity* ~ (Textbook p. 162)

Name _____

And Now the Good News

GRAPHIC ORGANIZER

Organizing Facts

The author goes on to say, "When we protect one habitat, we help all the animals that live there." The National Wildlife Refuge System cares for 400 habitats! In the circles of the diagram below, write the names of five creatures protected by the system.

Unit Two: *Clarity* ~ (Textbook p. 162) 55

Eddie, Incorporated

VOCABULARY — Activity 1

| chute | composed | efficiently | financial | transactions |
| competently | contracts | executive | income | vertical |

1. The "cousins club" was _____ (made up of) of girls who were not really cousins at all, but were five very close friends.

2. The club's top _____ (a person who has a position of leadership in a business or company) called the meeting to order.

3. "Girls," she said, "our problem is _____ (relating to money matters) or, in simpler terms, we need MONEY!"

4. "As you know, we all want to go to sleepaway camp this summer. However, not all our parents have a large enough _____ (the money an individual or business makes during a given time period) to pay for this terrific plan."

5. "It is up to us to solve this problem _____ (doing something with little or no waste of time and effort). Any ideas?"

6. "Come on, girls, I want to see those arms raised in a _____ (going up and down, not from side to side) position!"

7. "I have an idea," offered Hannah. "It involves small business _____ (buying or selling something) between us and our neighbors."

8. "What do you have in mind?" asked Miriam. "I think we're too young to be signing any _____ (written agreements between two parties)."

9. "Don't worry," laughed Hannah. "I just mean we should sell candy to our friends and neighbors. I think that's something we can do well and _____ (doing something in a good, but not outstanding way)."

10. "My brother and his friends sold candy last year. Mr. Roberts let them go to the basement of his store and pick up boxes of candy that had been delivered through the delivery _____ (a sloping passageway for delivering items from a higher to a lower level). After they sold the candy, they paid Mr. Roberts his share and kept the rest for themselves. I'm sure he'll let us do the same thing this year!"

Unit Three: Head, Hands, Heart ~ (Textbook p. 188)

Eddie, Incorporated

VOCABULARY

Activity II

Name _____

Helen was the Information Lady at a big bank. All day long people stood in line, waiting to ask her questions. At night she was so tired, she would fall asleep almost before her head hit the pillow. One night, her head was so full of questions and answers that she felt it would explode. She fell asleep and dreamed of questions and answers—but they were all mixed up! Hard as she tried, she could not match the answers to the questions! Can you help her?

Next to each question, put the letter of the answer that goes with it.

1. Who is the chief **executive** of this bank? _____

2. I noticed an opening near the ground that is boarded up. What was it used for? _____

3. What sort of **transactions** can your bank help me with? _____

4. Do you deal with other matters, such as education or politics? _____

5. I need help writing a **contract**. Whom should I ask? _____

6. Could you help me read this report from the bank? I'm not sure whether the numbers go up and down or left to right. _____

7. Can you help me with this form? It asks for my **income**. What should I include? _____

8. I'm not very good at numbers. Do you think I can handle my own bank account? _____

9. What is the most **efficient** way to pay my bills? _____

10. Is this the kind of question your dreams are always **composed** of? _____

Answers:
   a. We can help you with buying a home or starting a business.
   b. Write down your yearly salary plus any money that you earn some other way.
   c. Mr. Jackson.
   d. To draw up a written agreement you need a lawyer.
   e. It used to be a coal **chute**.
   f. The numbers are written in a **vertical** column and should be read that way.
   g. The bank recommends our computerized service if you wish to save time and energy.
   h. No, we deal only with **financial** matters.
   i. If you can add and subtract **competently**, you should be fine.
   j. Oh no! I usually dream of strawberry ice cream and sunny beaches.

Unit Three: *Head, Hands, Heart* ~ (Textbook p. 188)

Eddie, Incorporated

COMPREHENSION Questions

In-Depth Thinking

1. At the end of the story, how had Eddie's outlook on the business changed from what it was at the beginning of the story?

   _____
   _____
   _____

2. Explain the difference between a worker who earns a salary and a worker who receives a share of the profits.

   _____
   _____
   _____
   _____

3. How did each member of Eddie's family contribute to the Anselmino Aluminum Recycling Company?

   _____
   _____
   _____

Drawing Conclusions

4. How do you know that Eddie, Elizabeth, and Dink were all very eager and excited to start their business on Saturday?

   _____
   _____

Unit Three: Head, Hands, Heart ~ (Textbook p. 188)

Name _____

Eddie, Incorporated
COMPREHENSION
Questions

5. Why do you think schoolchildren would ruin posters, taunt others, or throw rocks down the chute?

_____
_____
_____

6. As you read the story, did you think the business was going to be a success? Why or why not? Was it successful in the end?

_____
_____
_____

One Step Further

Write about a business that you would like to open. Include details of the service you would provide, what supplies you would need, and why you think it would be successful. Remember that teamwork is very important to the success of any group or company. What qualities would you look for in your employees? What rules would you make to encourage your company members to work well together? What would you do if someone did not work well in a group?

_____
_____
_____
_____
_____
_____
_____
_____

Unit Three: *Head, Hands, Heart* ~ (Textbook p. 188)

Eddie, Incorporated

GRAPHIC ORGANIZER
Noticing a Plot's Detail

Any project requires a lot of work. While most of the work can be divided up before the project starts, there are always many small jobs that people must take on once the project has started. In *Eddie, Incorporated*, all three "bosses" are willing to pitch in to make their business a success.

The grid below, when completed, shows which jobs were taken on by each child. Every job, large or small, mentioned in the story is listed. Next to each job, write the name of the person who did it.

Was it Eddie, Dink, or Elizabeth?

painted a big OPEN sign	
kept a notebook listing expenses	
closed the basement window and removed the OPEN sign	

Unit Three: *Head, Hands, Heart* ~ (Textbook p. 188)

Name _____

Eddie, Incorporated

GRAPHIC ORGANIZER

Noticing a Plot's Detail

got there at 8:30 in case there was a line	
collected cans in his father's garbage can carrier	
put advertisement posters on poles	
washed and dried the cans	
made a night deposit box	
weighed the cans	

Unit Three: Head, Hands, Heart ~ (Textbook p. 188)

Heatwave!

VOCABULARY
Activity 1

| affected | commotion | horizon | plucking | trough |
| churned | herded | miscalculated | singe | whiff |

1. Mr. Stuart got out of his car. As far as the eye could see, there was corn. Corn, corn, corn, stretched all the way to the _____ (*the place in the distance where the earth and sky seem to meet*). And then, nothing but sky.

2. He had badly _____ (*judged incorrectly*) the distance between the town he had just left and the big city. Now, he was out of gas.

3. He hadn't eaten since the morning, and he was afraid his judgment was being _____ (*influenced*) by his hunger and weakness.

4. Suddenly, he heard a lot of noise. There seemed to be quite a _____ (*noise and disturbance*) somewhere in the fields, but he couldn't see anything.

5. Then, a smell, just a _____ (*slight smell*), of "cow" reached his nose.

6. Far away, he saw a barefoot boy and watched as a big dog _____ (*drove or led*) a group of cows in one direction.

7. "There must be a farm nearby," he said to himself. As he hurried towards the boy, he saw the farmhouse. In the yard, he saw a girl working and humming as she _____ (*shook and beat milk to turn it into butter*).

8. A few horses were drinking water out of a _____ (*a long, boxlike container used to hold food or water for animals*).

9. "Hello there," he said. "Do you have any gasoline for my car?" he asked the girl. Without answering she pointed to the backyard where, I saw, a lady was _____ (*pulling out*) the feathers off a chicken.

10. "Have you got any gas you could spare?" I asked the lady. "Sure do," she said, as she walked over to a little fire she had burning and held the plucked chicken over it. "Just wait 'til I _____ (*to burn slightly*) the rest of these feathers off the chicken and I'll get it for you." As I was thanking her, the girl ran up to me with a plate full of bread and freshly churned butter. "Have some," she said. "You look mighty hungry." I was, so I did!

Unit Three: Head, Hands, Heart ~ (Textbook p. 214)

Name _____

Heatwave!

VOCABULARY

Activity 11

A Picture is Worth a Thousand Words!

Draw a line from the vocabulary word to the picture that illustrates it.

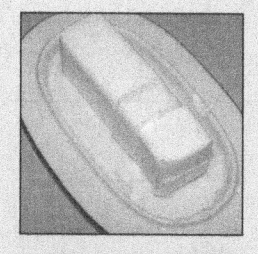

horizon

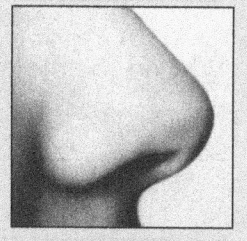

plucked

commotion

herded

churned

whiff

singe

trough

Write a sentence with each of the following words: **affected**; **miscalculated**.

_____

_____

_____

_____

Unit Three: Head, Hands, Heart ~ (Textbook p. 214) 63

Heatwave!

COMPREHENSION Questions

In-Depth Thinking

1. Why did the dog turn blue and freeze when he saw the popcorn?

2. Why do you think "Heat Wave" is capitalized in this story?

3. Did Hank's view of his sister change by the end of the story?

Drawing Conclusions

4. What conflicts were you able to identify in this story?

Unit Three: Head, Hands, Heart ~ (Textbook p. 214)

Name _____

Heatwave!

COMPREHENSION

Questions

5. The main character puts things into action quickly and is not easily discouraged. What other character traits does she have?

_____
_____
_____

6. Add one more item to the story and, keeping with the story's style, make something fantastic happen to it.

_____
_____
_____
_____

One Step Further

Necessity is the mother of invention.

In this story, the author comes up with ideas and solutions to help with the situation. Write about a certain issue that you or a family member have and a creative way to solve it.

_____
_____
_____
_____
_____
_____
_____

Unit Three: Head, Hands, Heart ~ (Textbook p. 214)

Heatwave!
GRAPHIC ORGANIZER
Writing Humor

In *Heatwave!*, we read about all kinds of weird and wonderful things that happen as a result of the extreme heat. Now, what happens to these same things when the weather turns extremely COLD? Under each phrase quoted from the story, write what happens when the weather is freezing. Then, in the box provided, draw a picture of what you described.

"A flock of geese flew in one side and came out the other side plucked, stuffed, and roasted."

_____

_____

_____

"The mercury blasted out of the porch thermometer like a rocket."

_____

_____

_____

"Ma's flowers pulled themselves up by their roots and crawled under the porch looking for shade."

_____

_____

_____

"The corn had started popping. It looked like a blizzard had hit."

_____

_____

_____

Unit Three: Head, Hands, Heart ~ (Textbook p. 214)

Name _____

Heatwave!
GRAPHIC ORGANIZER
Writing Humor

"The cows were hopping around like rabbits. The ground had gotten too hot..."

_____
_____
_____

"...the cows had jumped so much, they'd churned their milk to butter."

_____
_____
_____

"The cows were steaming, and their coats were starting to singe."

_____
_____
_____

"Those poor critters were about to cook!"

_____
_____
_____

"The bigger the [iceberg] lettuce grew, the cooler the air got."

_____
_____
_____

Unit Three: *Head, Hands, Heart* ~ (Textbook p. 214)　67

The Wright Brothers

COMPREHENSION Questions

In-Depth Thinking

1. What special qualities did Mrs. Wright have that influenced her sons so strongly?

2. What difference was there between the Wrights' sled and the ones that belonged to the other boys?

3. What role does wind resistance play in this story?

Drawing Conclusions

4. People said that Susan Wright spoiled her children by letting them do what they wanted. What did she really achieve by letting them do what they wanted?

Unit Three: Head, Hands, Heart ~ (Textbook p. 232)

Name _____

The Wright Brothers

COMPREHENSION

Questions

5. Why do you think the story begins with a conversation between Susan Wright and her sons about how birds fly?

_____
_____
_____

6. What kind of relationship did the Wright family members have with each other?

_____
_____
_____

One Step Further

The greatest good you can do for another is not just share your riches, but to reveal to him his own.
— Benjamin Disraeli

The word *riches* in this quote does not refer to money and wealth. What do you think it means? Write about a few of your own personal riches and a few of the riches of someone you know.

_____
_____
_____
_____
_____
_____
_____

Unit Three: *Head, Hands, Heart* ~ (Textbook p. 232)

The Wright Brothers

GRAPHIC ORGANIZER
Reading Comprehension

Mrs. Wright taught her sons many things about flight, speed, wind resistance, and making patterns. When the boys built their sled and, afterwards, when they raced with it, they remembered all those lessons. The result was the fastest sled and the speediest ride in the neighborhood!

1. "...the closer to the ground our sled is the less wind resistance there will be, and the faster it will go."

2. "You'd be surprised how much mothers know..."

3. "The narrower it is, the less wind resistance."

4. "If you get it right on paper, it'll be right when you build it."

5. "We rubbed the runners with the candles."

6. "...lie down on the sled...Less wind resistance this way..."

7. Less resistance from the snow on the ground.

Unit Three: Head, Hands, Heart ~ (Textbook p. 232)

Name _____

The Wright Brothers

GRAPHIC ORGANIZER

Reading Comprehension

On this page there is a drawing of a sled. Several features of the sled are pointed out. Choose the sentence from the opposite page that explains why the sled was built this way. Write the number of the sentence on the line provided.

Runners are smooth
_____

Built according to the pattern we drew first
_____

Mother showed us how
_____

Sled is narrow
_____

Boys will ride it lying down on their stomachs
_____

Thin runners
_____

Low to the ground
_____

Unit Three: *Head, Hands, Heart* ~ (Textbook p. 232)   71

The Imperfect/Perfect Book Report

COMPREHENSION Questions

In-Depth Thinking

1. Compare how Cricket felt about Zoe at the beginning of the story to the way she felt about her at the end of the story.

   _____
   _____
   _____

2. Do you think that Zoe had any idea of what Cricket was thinking all along?

   _____
   _____
   _____

3. In what ways will the students in Mrs. Schraalenburgh's class perform differently for the next book report?

   _____
   _____
   _____

Drawing Conclusions

4. Was Mrs. Schraalenburgh a good teacher? Explain why you think she was or wasn't.

   _____
   _____
   _____
   _____

Name _____

The Imperfect/Perfect Book Report

COMPREHENSION

Questions

5. Why do you think Cricket was careless when writing certain information in her report and extremely careful about other parts of her report?

_____

_____

_____

6. If you were in Julio's class, how would you feel about the A he got on his report?

_____

_____

_____

One Step Further

Competition is a painful thing but it produces great results.

Do you enjoy competition or dislike it? When is it a good thing and when is it not? What can one gain or lose from being competitive? What is your opinion? Write about it!

_____

_____

_____

_____

_____

_____

_____

_____

Unit Three: *Head, Hands, Heart* ~ (Textbook p. 252)

The Imperfect/Perfect Book Report

GRAPHIC ORGANIZER
Writing a Book Report

This story is about Cricket Kaufman and a book report she wrote. In the following exercise, you will write a "story report" on this story! Answer the guide questions. When you have written all the answers, you will have a report about this story.

Instructions:

Write the title of the story at the top of the page. Write the word "by" followed by the author's name on the next line. Skip a line and write "Reviewed by" and your name. Skip another line and begin to write your report by answering the questions that follow. Write in complete sentences, so that the answers will form three paragraphs.

- Who is the main character, what grade is she in, and what kind of student is she?
- Who is the other girl in the story, and what is her connection to the main character?
- Who is Mrs. Schraalenburgh? What makes her different from other teachers?
- You may now write your own opinion of Mrs. Schraalenburgh.
- Start a new paragraph. What assignment is given to the class?
- Describe the way Cricket does the assignment and add your explanation of why she works that way.
- What grade does Cricket think she will get?
- Who gets a good grade and why is Cricket surprised that he does?
- You may write what you think about the grade this student gets. Do you think he should have gotten that grade or not?
- What grade does Cricket get, and what are the comments the teacher makes?
- Start a new paragraph. What lessons does Cricket learn from her experience?
- Did you enjoy the story? Why or why not?
- The End

Unit Three: Head, Hands, Heart ~ (Textbook p. 252)

Name _____

The Imperfect/Perfect Book Report

GRAPHIC ORGANIZER
Writing a Book Report

Unit Three: Head, Hands, Heart ~ (Textbook p. 252)   75

The Imperfect/Perfect Book Report

GRAPHIC ORGANIZER
Writing a Book Report

Name _____

The Imperfect/Perfect Book Report
GRAPHIC ORGANIZER
Writing a Book Report

Justin Lebo

VOCABULARY — Activity 1

> battered   inspired   passion   proposal   semicircular
> gingerly   interchangeable   pirouettes   realigned   tooling

1. John Hanson, in his _____ (damaged by rough treatment) old hat, wrinkled suit, and scuffed shoes did not look like he would be a very interesting teacher.

2. On the first day of our astronomy class, he turned towards the blackboard and _____ (with great care) pulled down a white screen.

3. Once the lights were out, and the slide show had begun, the quiet, shy man began to speak with excitement and _____ (an enthusiasm for something).

4. On the screen was a picture of the sky in mid-summer. All across the top was the curved, _____ (shaped like half of a circle) Milky Way, looking like an arch, or bridge across the sky.

5. "Just look at those moons circling Jupiter!" he exclaimed. "Why, they look like they're doing _____ (a dance step in which the dancer twirls about on one foot) right around that planet!"

6. "And look at that shooting star, just _____ (driving or riding in a vehicle) across space!"

7. "Now what about that Pluto? Don't you think it's out of line and needs to be _____ (to return to the proper position) with the planet next to it?"

8. Mr. Hanson then turned on the lights. "I have a _____ (a suggested plan) for you."

9. "I would like our class to build a model of the solar system with parts that are moveable and _____ (two things that can be used in place of one another), so that we can keep moving the stars and planets around in our classroom as they move around in the sky throughout the school year."

10. As the year went by, that man in the old hat and wrinkled suit so _____ (filled with a sense of purpose) our class that many of us went on to become scientists, and I, myself, became an astronomer.

Unit Three: Head, Hands, Heart ~ (Textbook p. 268)

Who? What? Where? When? Why? And How?

1. *Where* would you wear your **battered** hat?
   a. to a family picnic and baseball game
   b. to an elegant wedding reception

2. *What* are you more likely to have a **passion** for?
   a. calcium with vitamin D in pill form
   b. chocolate ice cream with whipped cream

3. *What*, on your family's car, might need to be **realigned**?
   a. the paint job
   b. the wheels

4. *Who* might you see **tooling** around?
   a. a little boy on a bike
   b. a handyman repairing your roof

5. *Why* would one want a **semicircular** driveway?
   a. so that a driver does not need to back out
   b. so that the surface will never need fixing

6. *Who* can be seen doing **pirouettes**?
   a. a musician
   b. a dancer

7. *How* can you tell if two parts are **interchangeable**?
   a. if the instructions tell you they are
   b. if the instructions warn you not to use one part in place of another

8. *Where* would one hear a **proposal**?
   a. on a radio station that plays old favorites
   b. in a meeting of people looking for a new idea for their business

9. *What* would you handle **gingerly**?
   a. a football
   b. a rattlesnake

10. *Why* might you feel **inspired**?
    a. because you just heard a good speech
    b. because you just caught the flu

Justin Lebo

COMPREHENSION Questions

In-Depth Thinking

1. How did Justin's parents help him with his project?

2. How do you know that Justin was a good businessman?

3. How and why do you think the relationship between Justin and Mel changed over the course of the story?

Drawing Conclusions

4. What problem caused Justin to start the bicycle project?

Unit Three: *Head, Hands, Heart* ~ (Textbook p. 268)

Name _____

Justin Lebo
COMPREHENSION
Questions

5. Do you think Justin's behavior was typical for a ten year old? Why or why not?

_____

_____

_____

6. How do you think Justin's friends, neighbors, or reporters were affected by his answer to the popular question, "Why do you do this?"

_____

_____

_____

One Step Further

Justin said, "I don't think you can ever really do anything to help anybody else if it doesn't make you happy."

Write about what you think Justin means by this.

_____

_____

_____

_____

_____

_____

_____

_____

_____

Unit Three: Head, Hands, Heart ~ (Textbook p. 268)

Justin Lebo

GRAPHIC ORGANIZER
Reviewing Plot

Justin Lebo is a wonderful person. At a very young age he already knew the meaning of giving. He gave of his time, his money, his effort, and his skill. But Justin could not have succeeded alone. He was helped by many people. They wanted to help him because he was so unselfish and so enthusiastic. He gave them the opportunity to do good, and they gave him help, advice, and support.

In the exercise below, each bicycle represents one person who helped Justin. In the space provided, describe the type of help each character provided.

Mr. Lebo

How Mr. Lebo Helped
_____
_____
_____

Mrs. Lebo

How Mrs. Lebo Helped
_____
_____
_____

Unit Three: Head, Hands, Heart ~ (Textbook p. 268)

Name _____

Justin Lebo

GRAPHIC ORGANIZER

Reviewing Plot

A Neighbor	How the Neighbor Helped

A Reporter	How the Reporter Helped

Readers of the Article	How the Readers of the Article Helped

The "Kid" at the End of the Story	How the Kid at the End of the Story Helped

Unit Three: *Head, Hands, Heart* ~ (Textbook p. 268)

Earthquake Terror

VOCABULARY
Activity 1

| bolted | engrossed | impact | meandered | stifling |
| cataloging | evaporated | jarring | relinquish | susceptible |

1. It was Sunday, and I was _____ (completely involved in) in my favorite pastime.

2. I was _____ (organizing into groups) my baseball cards, the ones with the old-time greats, the all-star players of the '20s, '30s, and '40s.

3. It was a warm, humid day, and if I had not been so fascinated by the job I was doing, I would have felt the air was _____ (hot and still).

4. I was beginning to feel drowsy. My eyelids were drooping when, suddenly, I felt something _____ (shaking) the couch I was sitting on.

5. I looked up and, much to my astonishment, I saw the great Babe Ruth standing in the room. He was holding onto his bat, as if to say he would not _____ (let go of) it.

6. I was further amazed when a baseball came sailing through the open window. BAM—the _____ (the force with which one thing hits another) of Ruth's bat slamming the ball sounded like an explosion.

7. A second later, Babe Ruth _____ (suddenly ran away) from the room, probably on his way to first base—wherever that was!

8. I jumped up to look out the window but Babe, his bat, and the ball had all gone, as if they had _____ (disappeared).

9. I had never thought I was _____ (likely to be affected by) to hallucinations, so I realized that this was a dream.

10. The next day, as I _____ (winded gently from one place to another) around my yard, I noticed some footprints in the mud. Who'd been there the day before, I wondered. Hmmm....

Unit Four: *Caring* ~ (Textbook p. 326)

Earthquake Terror

VOCABULARY — Activity 1

Name _____

| debris | dwarfed | pungent | suspended | upheaval |
| devastation | ominous | retreated | undulating | wedged |

1. Captain Barkley walked carefully into the deserted town and saw total _____ (*destruction and ruin*).

2. The enemy had _____ (*moved back*) to the forest around the city, but he could almost feel their presence.

3. All around were stones, bricks, and other _____ (*remains of anything destroyed*) caused by the shooting and shelling of the previous day.

4. The fighting had been _____ (*temporarily stopped*) for a while, as both sides gathered their wounded soldiers and tried to prepare for another battle.

5. The skies were gray and _____ (*threatening*), the perfect backdrop to this scene of destruction and misery.

6. Captain Barkley looked up and saw one of his men, Thompson, _____ (*appeared small by comparison*) by a huge pile of rubble he was searching.

7. As the captain approached Thompson, a _____ (*sharp and strong*) smell reached his nose.

8. Looking for the source of the smell, he saw a small dog pulling at something that was _____ (*packed in tightly*) between two bricks.

9. Walking away from the dog and the smell, Captain Barkley thought of the days before this terrible war had created such an _____ (*a great disturbance*) in his life.

10. He daydreamed about the summer days he used to spend walking beside the gently _____ (*moving with a wavelike motion*) waters of the river near his home.

Unit Four: *Caring* ~ (Textbook p. 326)

Earthquake Terror

VOCABULARY
Activity II

Usage

Have you ever tried to peel a potato with a hammer? Have you ever tried to dig up a worm with a ladle? We hope not! You need the right tool for each job. The same is true in language. You need the right word for the sentence, and the right sentence for the word. In the following exercise, a vocabulary word is used correctly in one of the sentences. Circle the sentence in which the word is used correctly.

Which sentence is correct?

1. a. The librarian was sitting there, *evaporating* the books.
   b. The librarian was sitting there, *cataloging* the books.

2. a. The vibrations from his loud boom box were actually *jarring* the crystal glasses that stood delicately on the shelf.
   b. The vibrations from his boom box were actually *engrossing* the crystal glasses that stood delicately on the shelf.

3. a. The *bolting* of the car hitting the pole caused the windshield to shatter.
   b. The *impact* of the car hitting the pole caused the windshield to shatter.

4. a. He is very *engrossed* in colds.
   b. He is very *susceptible* to colds.

5. a. The baby would not *relinquish* the rattle.
   b. The baby would not *bolt* the rattle.

6. a. The gentle brook *bolted* through the valley.
   b. The gentle brook *meandered* through the valley.

7. a. The *stifling* room made us feel faint.
   b. The *jarring* room made us feel faint.

8. a. When the lightning struck, the horse *bolted* from the barn.
   b. When the lightning struck, the horse *meandered* from the barn.

9. a. The window broke from the *impact* of the hail.
   b. The window broke from the *stifling* of the hail.

10. a. The student, *relinquishing* the book, didn't give it back.
    b. The student, *engrossed* in the book, didn't give it back.

Earthquake Terror

VOCABULARY

Activity II

Name _____

Left Out!

| debris | dwarfed | pungent | suspended | upheaval |
| devastation | ominous | retreated | undulating | wedged |

The following exercise is a little tricky. Each sentence is written with one of the vocabulary words in mind. The overall meaning of the sentence is the **opposite** of the meaning of the word. You would *never* use that vocabulary word in a sentence like this! Next to each sentence, circle the vocabulary word that is most opposite in meaning to what the sentence is about.

Example: Napoleon's armies fought fiercely. They had victory after victory. They marched from one country to another, winning every battle.   <u>retreated</u> • undulating

1. Oh, what a beautiful morning it was! The sun was shining, the sky was blue, and we just knew the day would be wonderful. **upheaval** • **ominous**

2. We called the phone company to find out if our service had been restored. They told us the bill had been paid and our phones would be working from now on. **suspended** • **retreated**

3. The plate cracked because it had been packed too loosely in the box. **wedged** • **dwarfed**

4. I had never seen a road so straight and flat. It seemed to go for miles without curving at all. **dwarfed** • **undulating**

5. It was early spring and the trees had tiny buds on them. There was just the slightest hint of fragrance in the air. **retreated** • **pungent**

6. We saw a herd of black stallions. All of them appeared large and powerful. **dwarfed** • **debris**

7. The town was bustling. Everywhere, new buildings, lush gardens, and dazzling displays met the eye. **devastation** • **suspended**

8. Let me tell you about my hometown. It is the dullest, most boring place you can imagine. Nothing has changed there in fifty years. **undulating** • **upheaval**

9. The place where the fire was had been completely cleaned up. There was not one single reminder that this field had once been the location of a big department store. **debris** • **ominous**

Unit Four: *Caring* ~ (Textbook p. 326)   87

Earthquake Terror

COMPREHENSION Questions

In-Depth Thinking

1. What were some hints that an earthquake was on the way?

   _____
   _____
   _____
   _____

2. Why was Moose much more than 'just' a pet to Jonathan?

   _____
   _____
   _____
   _____

3. Compare Jonathan to Abby. List two ways in which they are different and two ways in which they are the same.

   _____
   _____
   _____
   _____
   _____
   _____

Drawing Conclusions

4. What information did Jonathan use on that day that he had not needed any other time?

   _____
   _____
   _____
   _____

Name _____

Earthquake Terror

COMPREHENSION
Questions

5. In describing his feelings, Jonathan sometimes compared the way he felt at that moment to the way he felt in a different situation. For example, to describe how slowly the time seemed to be moving, he talked about the way a person feels waiting in the dentist's office. What are two other places where he used comparisons to describe his feelings?

_____
_____
_____

6. Do you think Jonathan was a good brother?

_____
_____

One Step Further

Bravery is being the only one who knows you're afraid. — Franklin P. Jones

It's easy to be brave from a distance. — Aesop

Think about the meaning of these two quotes. Do you agree or disagree with them? Make up a little story about an ordinary person who is suddenly faced with a challenge. Write an internal dialogue for this character, which tells the reader what the person's thoughts were before, during, and after he or she met the challenge courageously.

_____
_____
_____
_____
_____
_____
_____

Unit Four: *Caring* ~ (Textbook p. 326)

Earthquake Terror

GRAPHIC ORGANIZER
Identifying Clues

After we learn that Jonathan and Abby have been left alone in the woods, the author begins to give the reader clues about what is to come. Below is a list of five clues about the upcoming earthquake. The clues are not listed in the correct order. On this page and the next, there are five magnifying glasses. Write one clue into each magnifying glass. Put them in the proper order. (You may wish to number them before you copy them into the magnifying glasses.)

___ "He heard a deep rumbling sound in the distance."

___ "Moose suddenly stood still, his legs stiff and his tail up."

___ "Another loud noise exploded as Jonathan lurched sideways."

___ "Moose barked...his warning bark, the one he used when a stranger knocked on the door."

___ "No magpies cawed, no leaves rustled overhead."

Unit Four: *Caring* ~ (Textbook p. 326)

Name _____

Earthquake Terror

GRAPHIC ORGANIZER

Identifying Clues

Unit Four: *Caring* ~ (Textbook p. 326)

91

The Gift

VOCABULARY
Activity 1

| balmy | glistened | linger | monologue | scavenging |
| console | haltingly | luminous | propelled | wan |

1. Amy lived in a cottage near the seashore. All summer, she would watch the tourists take advantage of the near perfect, _____ (*mild and refreshing*) weather.

2. All sorts of people walked on the beach. Some walked _____ (*slowly, with hesitation*), stopping every moment to look for seashells.

3. Others, especially children, ran about as though they were _____ (*moved, driven*) by some little motor inside of them.

4. Sometimes, Amy would see a person who looked _____ (*pale and weak*).

5. She would wish she could go up to the person and _____ (*comfort*) him.

6. In her mind, she would make a little talk, a _____ (*a speech made by one person with no answer from the listener*), in which she said just the right words to cheer the person up. Of course, she never did this, because her mother had warned her not to talk to strangers.

7. Sometimes, she would see people _____ (*taking or gathering something useable from among unwanted things*), looking for treasures in the sand.

8. Whenever they saw something that glittered or _____ (*shone*), they would pounce on it, hoping it was buried treasure.

9. Amy would smile to herself because she had never seen anyone find anything of value in the sand. What was valuable to her was the pure white light of the _____ (*reflecting light*) moon, which sent dancing sunbeams to play on the sand after the sun had set.

10. On clear nights, she would _____ (*stay longer than necessary because one does not want to leave*) on the beach long after the last of the tourists had gone home, admiring the moon, the stars, and the sand, and the quiet peace of the sea.

Unit Four: Caring ~ (Textbook p. 350)

The Gift

VOCABULARY

Activity II

Name _____

Shades of Meaning

The world we live in is full of color, and those colors come in every shade. Feelings that we have, or people that we know, are like that, too. They come in "shades." Words help us express the small differences that exist in our world.

For example, sometimes you are hungry. Other times, you are very, very hungry. You would probably say, "I'm starving!" We might say:

starving = hungry + very

Many of your vocabulary words can be broken down the same way. For example, to **linger** means not just "to remain in one place"; it means "to remain in one place *longer* than one needs to."

In the exercise below, each vocabulary word is given, with part of its definition. In the box at the bottom, there is a group of words that add the "shading" to each definition. Choose the phrase from the box that completes the definition of each vocabulary word and write it on the line.

balmy = mild weather _____

glistened = shone _____

haltingly = slowly _____

linger = to remain in one place _____

luminous = reflecting light _____

monologue = a speech by one person _____

propelled = was moved _____

scavenging = looking for something of worth _____

wan = pale _____

```
longer than is necessary
by some other force
and sickly looking
that is warm and refreshing
among mostly useless items
in a soft, moonlike glow
and sparkled in the light
with small stops along the way
when the listener or listeners do not interrupt
```

Unit Four: *Caring* ~ (Textbook p. 350)

The Gift

COMPREHENSION Questions

In-Depth Thinking

1. Why did Nana Marie and Anna become friends?

   _____
   _____
   _____

2. Compare the way Nana Marie behaved to Anna to the way Rita behaved towards her.

   _____
   _____
   _____

3. Nana Marie taught Anna a special way to see the world. To Nana Marie, every object had a story. Anna saw many things during her day in the woods. Choose one thing she saw, and describe it as if you are talking to Nana Marie.

   _____
   _____
   _____
   _____

Drawing Conclusions

4. Do you think the gifts the other people gave Nana Marie were as thoughtful as the gift Anna gave her?

   _____
   _____
   _____

Name _____

The Gift

COMPREHENSION

Questions

5. Do you think it is unusual for a young girl to befriend an older lady?

_____
_____
_____

6. Why would Nana Marie remember this day more than any other, perhaps more than the day she lost her sight?

_____
_____
_____

One Step Further

The only way to have a friend is to be one. — Ralph Waldo Emerson

Do you think that the above quote is true? Explain why or why not.

_____
_____
_____
_____
_____
_____
_____
_____
_____

The Gift

GRAPHIC ORGANIZER
Using Descriptive Language

"You didn't have a last day to look at the world," Anna said. "So I brought it to you. Everything I saw today. Just as if you saw it with me. The way you would see it. And tomorrow I'll bring you another— and the next day another."

How did Anna describe what she had seen? Anna used **descriptive language**. She didn't say "I saw the mist." She said "I saw...the yellow mist breathing in and out."

In the following exercise, the word Anna is describing is underlined. Circle the descriptive words. The first one is done for you.

1. "Ahead was a place she often came, a (small, deep) spring in the woods."

2. "When she knelt to gaze into the bottomless pool, at first she saw nothing but darkness."

3. "Then as the sun came out, the water seemed to open up, reflecting the bark of silver beeches, shining like armor."

4. "...her sneakers were wet from the soft thawing soil of the woods..."

5. "The wan February sun was swallowed by a thick mist..."

6. "Although the air was damp, it had an edge of warmth that had been absent in the morning."

In the gift boxes, write a description of the object or activity named. Follow the instructions for the type of description you should write.

The first one is done for you.

> We bumped along in the old yellow bus, children popping up and down like popcorn in an air popper.

Anna wishes to describe the ride in the school bus.

Unit Four: *Caring* ~ (Textbook p. 350)

Name _____

The Gift

GRAPHIC ORGANIZER
Using Descriptive Language

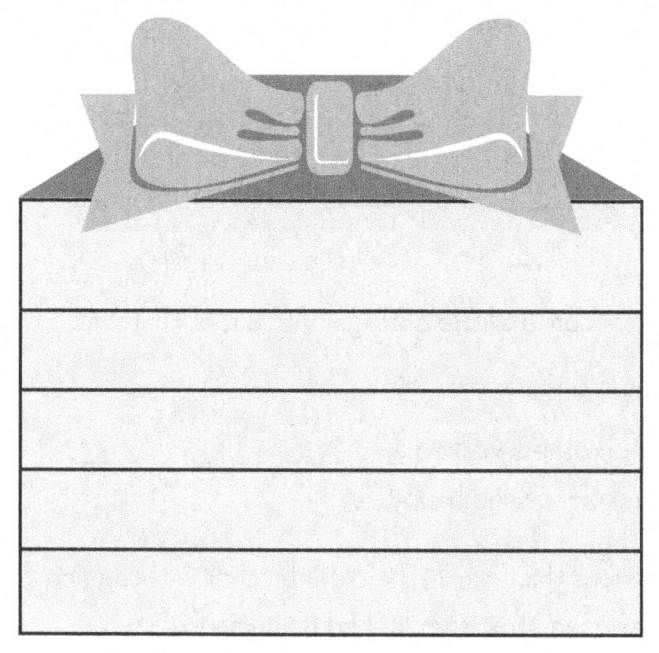

The pizza deliveryman slipping on the ice.
Describe the smell and warmth of the pizza.
Use humor to describe what happens.

The autumn leaves.
Describe the color, smell,
and sound of the leaves.

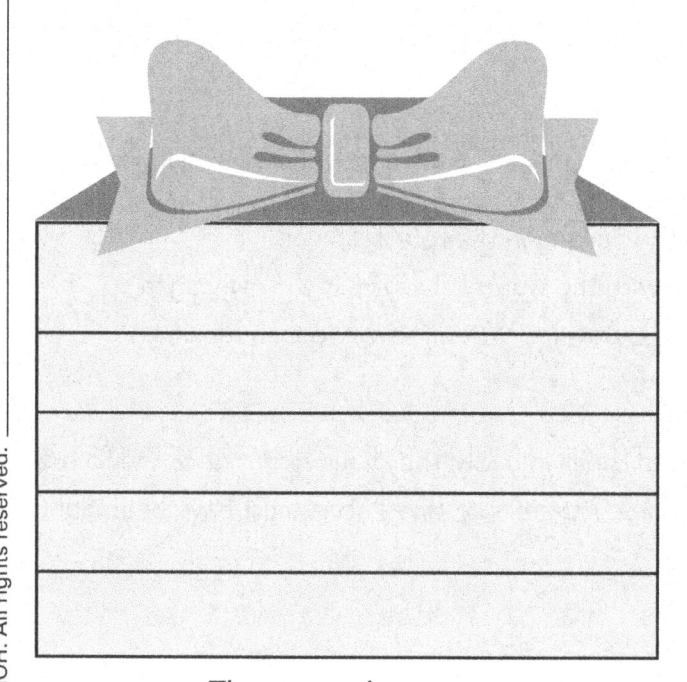

The winning home run.
Describe the ball's movement, the sound of
the bat, and the reaction of the crowd.

The new kitten.
Describe how it feels, sounds, and moves.

Unit Four: *Caring* ~ (Textbook p. 350)   97

Toto

VOCABULARY — Activity 1

| crude | jauntily | mock | poachers | thatched |
| doused | menacing | plains | snare | timid |

1. Once upon a time there was a shy, _____ (easily frightened) little girl who lived near a forest.

2. She lived with her parents and two older brothers in a pretty little cottage with a roof that was _____ (roof made of straw).

3. She would watch out the window every day as her brothers walked _____ (lively, slightly proud way) into the forest, looking carefree and happy.

4. One day, her brothers came home looking more serious than usual. The older brother was carrying a rough, _____ (not well-designed) trap that looked homemade.

5. "It looks like there are _____ (people who hunt or fish in an area where they are not allowed) at work in the forest, hunting the king's deer and trampling on his plants," he said.

6. "Look at this _____ (trap) that I found," he said, waving it in the air.

7. "I don't like the idea of strangers hurting and _____ (threatening) the animals in the forest."

8. "This is no child's _____ (pretend) trap; it is a real one that can injure or kill."

9. The father entered, looking exhausted. "I saw a fire burning in the forest. I _____ (threw water on) it with the water I always carry in my wagon, thinking it was caused by lightning or some careless traveler. When I saw two men running, I realized it had been set by some poachers."

10. "Papa," the little girl said, "if I know you, you scared them so badly, they'll run right out of the forest all the way to the _____ (large flat areas of land)!" She must have been right, because they never saw those two thieves again.

Unit Four: Caring ~ (Textbook p. 368)

Name _____

Toto

VOCABULARY

Activity II

Would You...?

Circle the correct answer.

1. **thatch**
   a. a baseball or
   b. a cottage

2. put a **poacher** in
   a. a frying pan or
   b. jail

3. **jauntily**
   a. walk down the lane or
   b. move a boulder out of the path

4. feel **timid** when
   a. facing the principal or when
   b. calling your best friend

5. describe a **plain** as
   a. twisty and curvy or as
   b. flat and boring

6. **douse**
   a. a glass of water or
   b. a little fire

7. lay a **snare** for
   a. hot dogs or for
   b. squirrels

8. use a **crude** instrument to
   a. break a rock into many small pieces or to
   b. remove an appendix

9. try to look **menacing** in front of
   a. a librarian or
   b. a robber

10. fight a **mock** battle with
    a. your friend or
    b. your enemy

Unit Four: *Caring* ~ (Textbook p. 368)   99

Toto

COMPREHENSION Questions

In-Depth Thinking

1. How were Suku and Toto each different from others their age?

   _____
   _____
   _____

2. How do you think Suku felt about the boys' teasing?

   _____
   _____
   _____

3. Suku and Toto had learned many lessons from their parents. What lessons helped them on the day they met?

   _____
   _____
   _____
   _____

Drawing Conclusions

4. Find three phrases in the story that tell the reader how Suku and Toto felt about one another.

   _____
   _____
   _____

5. Do you think Suku was brave? Why or why not? Do you think Suku thought of himself as brave?

   _____
   _____
   _____
   _____

Name _____

Toto
COMPREHENSION
Questions

6. How had Suku and Toto changed by the end of the story?

_____

_____

_____

One Step Further

If you don't risk anything, you risk even more. — Erica Jong

Only those who will risk going too far can possibly find out how far one can go.
— T. S. Elliot

Think about the above quotes. Your teacher will discuss them briefly with the class, then ask you to express in writing whether you agree or disagree with what they state.

_____

_____

_____

_____

_____

_____

_____

_____

_____

_____

_____

Unit Four: *Caring* ~ (Textbook p. 368)

Toto

GRAPHIC ORGANIZER
Using Venn Diagrams

Toto is the story of a boy, Suku, and an elephant, Toto. Although the two are very different, as an elephant and a boy must be, in some ways they are the same. In the Venn diagram on the opposite page, the center part will show how the boy and the elephant are the same, and the two outside sections will show how they are different. Fill out the diagram by putting the answers to the questions below into the correct section. If the answer is the same for both Suku and Toto, put it into the middle section. If the answers are different, put each answer into the correct outer section. Make sure you answer in complete sentences.

1. What country did Toto and Suku live in?
2. Where in the country did they live?
3. What could you see in the distance from their homes?
4. Were Toto and Suku old or young?
5. What did Toto and Suku learn that a growing boy or elephant needed to know?
6. Did their mothers want them to go far from home?
7. Did Toto and Suku want to go far from home?
8. Were Toto and Suku fearful?
9. Were Toto and Suku angry at the poachers?
10. Did Toto and Suku run when they saw the lion?
11. Did Toto and Suku change from the beginning to the end of the story?
12. Did Toto and Suku have someone older, who loved them, come to their rescue?

Name _____

Toto

GRAPHIC ORGANIZER

Using Venn Diagrams

Suku

Toto and Suku lived in Africa.

same

Toto

Unit Four: *Caring* ~ (Textbook p. 368)

Owl Moon

COMPREHENSION Questions

In-Depth Thinking

1. What was the narrator afraid of when she was owling?

   _____
   _____
   _____
   _____

2. What was it about owling that the narrator found exciting?

   _____
   _____
   _____
   _____

3. The poem often describes one thing by comparing it to another ("it was as quiet as a dream"). These comparisons are called similes. Find two other similes in the poem.

   _____
   _____

Drawing Conclusions

4. What are some ways to express a thought without speaking?

   _____
   _____
   _____
   _____

Name _____

Owl Moon

COMPREHENSION

Questions

5. At the end of the story the narrator says, "When you go owling you don't need words or warm or anything but hope." Why don't you need words? Why don't you need "warm"? What are you hoping for?

_____
_____
_____

6. Which part of the night's adventure do you think the narrator will remember for the longest time? Explain why you have selected that particular thing.

_____
_____
_____

One Step Further

Nature has been for me, as long as I remember…a home, a teacher, a companion.

— Lorraine Anderson

After discussing this quote with your teacher, write in what ways you think that nature can be a home, a teacher, and a companion.

_____
_____
_____
_____
_____
_____
_____

Unit Four: *Caring* ~ (Textbook p. 386)

Owl Moon

GRAPHIC ORGANIZER
Visual Images

Owl Moon is full of images. When you read them, the words become pictures in your imagination. Read the line from the poem that is written under each owl. What do you see in your imagination when you read that line? Draw a picture of the image inside the owl.

"The trees stood still as giant statues."

"They sang out, trains and dogs…"

"…little gray footprints followed us."

"…my short, round shadow bumped after me."

Unit Four: *Caring* ~ (Textbook p. 386)

Name _____

Owl Moon

GRAPHIC ORGANIZER

Visual Images

"...the line of pine trees, black and pointy against the sky..."

"The moon made his face into a silver mask."

"...as if someone's icy hand was palm-down on my back."

"...I was a shadow as we walked home."

Unit Four: *Caring* ~ (Textbook p. 386)

Homeward the Arrow's Flight

VOCABULARY
Activity 1

| allotment | consult | inundated | ominous | siege |
| appointment | grippe | lull | resentment | vicious |

1. Captain Morris paced back and forth, waiting for the train with the _____ *(the portion of something that is assigned to someone)* of bandages and medicine to arrive.

2. He was an army doctor stationed in France during the First World War, and many of the men in his company were sick with the _____ *(influenza)*.

3. He had been _____ *(flooded)* all day long with long lines of coughing, feverish men trying to see him.

4. It was winter and, in addition to fighting the enemy, the soldiers had had to fight a _____ *(a serious attack, as in illness)*, from pneumonia to strep.

5. Captain Morris had spent the previous year on an army base in Italy. He had been given this _____ *(position; job)* a month ago.

6. Already, he felt _____ *(a feeling of angry displeasure with someone)* toward his commanders for not supplying him with more medical equipment.

7. The weather was _____ *(harsh and cruel)*, and the men, already worn down from the war, were falling sick in great numbers.

8. Today, again, the gray sky looked angry and _____ *(threatening)*.

9. As the captain waited for the train to arrive, he decided that as soon as there was a _____ *(temporary calm)* in all the activity he would try to get some advice.

10. He decided he would _____ *(asking advice of)* the doctor in the nearby town about how best to treat the influenza with the little medicine that was available.

Unit Four: Caring ~ (Textbook p. 400)

Homeward the Arrow's Flight

VOCABULARY

Activity 1

Name _____

| agonized | consternation | don | maneuvered | ventured |
| confined | desolately | hoist | manipulate | wallow |

---

1. Mike thought he was not an animal. He really could not explain why he was behind bars, _____ *(restricted; kept from leaving a place)* to a cage.

2. He was not a sad little monkey—oh, no! He never _____ *(worried unhappily)* over the fact that he lived in a zoo.

3. He did not wish to cause the zookeepers any worry or _____ *(a sudden alarming amazement or dread)* at finding his cage empty.

4. He therefore _____ *(to go carefully into an unknown or dangerous place)* out of his cage only at night or on holidays when no one was about.

5. Whenever Mike felt adventurous, he would leap onto the shelf in his cage and _____ *(raise)* himself up to the window by a rope that hung from the ceiling.

6. What the zookeepers did not know was that Mike knew how to move and _____ *(handle with skill)* the bars on the window in a way that allowed him to squeeze through them.

7. Once out of his cage, Mike liked to visit the gift shop. There, he would pull on a zoo sweatshirt, _____ *(put on)* a colorful cap, and get ready for a good time!

8. On warm evenings, he would visit the sea lions and _____ *(roll about in a clumsy way)* in the water with them.

9. He would watch the elephants as they _____ *(moved about and changed direction as required)* around each other in their living area.

10. As the sun began to rise, he would _____ *(very sadly)* wave farewell to the other zoo animals and go back into his cage.

Unit Four: *Caring* ~ (Textbook p. 400)

Homeward the Arrow's Flight

VOCABULARY — Activity II

Answer This!

Write answers to the following questions, using the vocabulary word that is printed under each question. Your answers may be serious or funny, but they must show that you understand the meaning of the vocabulary word.

1. Was it easy for President Abraham Lincoln to make the decision to go to war with the South?

    agonized _____

2. "I'm glad to see you up and about. Were you sick for very long?"

    confined _____

3. "What were your parents' feelings when you told them you wished to become a lion tamer?"

    consternation _____

4. "When Nina told you she was moving, could you tell whether she was happy about the move?"

    desolately _____

5. "You know Jack—he refuses to wear anything but jeans. Did he get dressed up for the wedding?"

    donned _____

6. "However in the world did they get that statue all the way to the top of that building?"

    hoisted _____

7. "There are so many big rocks near the shore; how was that motorboat able to pick you up?"

    maneuvered _____

8. "I would love to drive one of those big machines they use to pave the road. What do you think I'd have to learn to get a job like that?"

    manipulate _____

9. "Tell me about your grandfather. Was he a stay-at-home person, or did he like to travel?"

    venture _____

10. How do the elephants keep cool in that hundred-degree heat?

    wallowed _____

Unit Four: *Caring* ~ (Textbook p. 400)

Alphabet Soup

| allotment | consult | inundated | ominous | siege |
| appointment | grippe | lull | resentment | vicious |

Did your mother ever tell you not to play with your food? Here's your chance to play with the words in your alphabet soup! Try to answer the questions below.

1. Which word contains something that you need on a pencil? _____

2. Which word has a sweet dried fruit in it? _____

3. Which word is half of what you would sing to a baby? _____

4. Unscramble this one: isuvico _____

5. Which word contains the answer you would give if your friend asked you how much whipped cream you wanted on your pie? _____

6. Which word has the letters of a fat, pink animal in it? _____

7. Which word has the letters that spell the sound a cow makes? _____

8. Which word has the letters that tell you how to find out how many dimes are in your pocket? _____

9. Which word has the letters that spell a place to sleep when you're camping out? _____

10. Subtract an "i" and add an "e" and you have some things that honk! _____

Homeward the Arrow's Flight

COMPREHENSION Questions

In-Depth Thinking

1. Compare what went on in Tom's house to what went on in the Whitefeather home.

2. What was sometimes neglected as a result of Susan's work? Why do you think this was so?

3. Who was Iron Eye and how did he inspire Susan?

Drawing Conclusions

4. What kind of relationship was there between Susan's family members?

Name _____

Homeward the Arrow's Flight

COMPREHENSION
Questions

5. How did the lesson from Susan's father, to accept change, apply to this selection?

_____
_____
_____

6. Susan felt guilty when she found Jimmy. Do you think she was at fault for making the wrong decision?

_____
_____
_____
_____

One Step Further

True strength lies in submission which permits one to dedicate his life, through devotion, to something beyond himself.
— Henry Miller

Explain what you think this quote means to you. Your teacher will define any difficult words. Do you agree with what this quote is saying?

_____
_____
_____
_____
_____
_____
_____
_____

Unit Four: *Caring* ~ (Textbook p. 400) 113

Homeward the Arrow's Flight

GRAPHIC ORGANIZER
Reviewing the Characters

When a story has many characters, it is sometimes difficult for the reader to remember who each one is. To help you, we have made some flash cards for review. The name of the character should be on one side of the card. Some important fact about or description of the character should be on the other side. However, only one side of each card is filled out! You must fill out the other side! Look back at the story to help you remember what each character did. The first set is done for you.

Susan La Flesche

The first female Native American doctor in the U.S.

[blank name card]

Susan's sister who lives on the reservation

Iron Eye

[blank description card]

[blank name card]

the Native Americans who lived on the reservation

Pie

[blank description card]

Unit Four: Caring ~ (Textbook p. 400)

Name _____

Homeward the Arrow's Flight

GRAPHIC ORGANIZER

Reviewing the Characters

Marguerite

Joe

He is married to Susan's sister Marguerite. He is very sick and doesn't make it through the winter.

Jimmy

Joe's wife. Susan comes through the storm to help her give birth.

Charlie's brother who comes for the funeral.

Unit Four: Caring ~ (Textbook p. 400)

Underwater Rescue

VOCABULARY — Activity 1

| abundantly | embedded | hovered | needlessly | reef |
| domain | enraged | instinctively | peer | shaft |

1. As our little boat sailed through the frigid water, our guide told us we were entering the _____ (*a region inhabited by a certain type of wildlife*) of the polar bear, where polar bears were king.

2. We turned towards the shore, our able captain steering his way around a _____ (*a ridge of rocks or sand near the surface of the water*) which stood between our boat and the shore.

3. Great chunks of ice floated around us. Sometimes we would see fish or other small creatures _____ (*set deeply into*) in the ice.

4. Suddenly, we heard a ghastly roar. On shore, we saw an _____ (*extremely angry*) polar bear on its hind legs, roaring in pain.

5. A hunter, who we could not see, had thrown a spear at him. The spear had pierced him so deeply that only its _____ (*the long, straight stem of something*) was visible.

6. Already, vultures _____ (*waited nearby*) overhead, waiting to see if the bear would die.

7. The bear managed to pull the spear out of his side. Then he _____ (*knowing what to do without thinking*) rolled in the snow, to stop the bleeding.

8. The captain _____ (*unnecessarily*) warned us not to approach the bear. He didn't have to worry; we knew to keep our distance.

9. It was _____ (*very much*) clear to us that we should not come anywhere near a polar bear, wounded or not.

10. As we stood watching from the safety of our boat, we saw another bear, his _____ (*one who the equal of another*) in size and ferociousness, approach him. This, we thought, must be Mrs. Bear, coming to help and heal him.

Name _____

Underwater Rescue

VOCABULARY

Activity II

If...

Circle the correct answer.

1. If your mother worried **needlessly** about your bike race, that means that
   a. you came home safe and sound.
   b. you fell off your bike and broke your leg.

2. If the lion was **enraged**, that explains why
   a. he dozed off in the hot sun.
   b. he roared and shook his mane.

3. If the captain spotted a **reef**, he would
   a. steer his boat away from it.
   b. catch it for his aquarium.

4. If the **shaft** of the knife is smooth
   a. the knife is easy to hold.
   b. the knife will not fall apart.

5. If the town has an **abundant** supply of water,
   a. the townspeople may use water freely.
   b. the townspeople must be very careful not to waste any water.

6. If we speak of a crocodile's **domain**, we are probably thinking of
   a. how dangerous he is.
   b. where he can usually be found.

7. If we see a mother bird **instinctively** feeding her young, we might say:
   a. "She is so kindhearted! She has such love for her young!"
   b. "Look how the mother bird just knows what to do for her young."

8. If a pearl is found **embedded** in an oyster
   a. it will easily roll right out.
   b. it will have to be pried out.

9. If seagulls **hover** above the water,
   a. people in a canoe will hardly be able to see them.
   b. people in a canoe can toss pieces of bread to them.

10. If a king wishes to speak to a **peer**,
    a. he must search for another king.
    b. he must search for the poorest man in his kingdom.

Unit Five: Determination ~ (Textbook p. 428)

Underwater Rescue

COMPREHENSION Questions

In-Depth Thinking

1. Why did Wayne want to help the dolphins? What made him hesitate to offer help?

   _____
   _____
   _____
   _____

2. How were the diver and the dolphins able to trust each other?

   _____
   _____
   _____
   _____

3. In your opinion, how did Wayne's feelings about dolphins change between the beginning of the story and the end?

   _____
   _____
   _____
   _____

Drawing Conclusions

4. Was Wayne afraid as the three dolphins approached him? Why or why not?

   _____
   _____
   _____

Name _____

Underwater Rescue

COMPREHENSION

Questions

5. In the beginning, the author hints that this will be an exciting story. What does he say?

_____
_____
_____

6. Do you think a situation like this one will occur again? Why or why not?

_____
_____
_____

One Step Further

The most important thing about communication is to hear what isn't being said. What do you think is meant by this quote?

_____
_____
_____
_____
_____
_____
_____
_____
_____

Unit Five: *Determination* ~ (Textbook p. 428)

Underwater Rescue

GRAPHIC ORGANIZER
Writing Dialogue

As we read *Underwater Rescue* we feel as though we are watching a pantomime. The diver and the dolphins communicate without words. But what if they could talk? What would they be saying? Each of the pictures below represents one event in the story. Read the quote from the story that is under each picture and write what you think each one was saying in the speech bubbles. The first one is done for you.

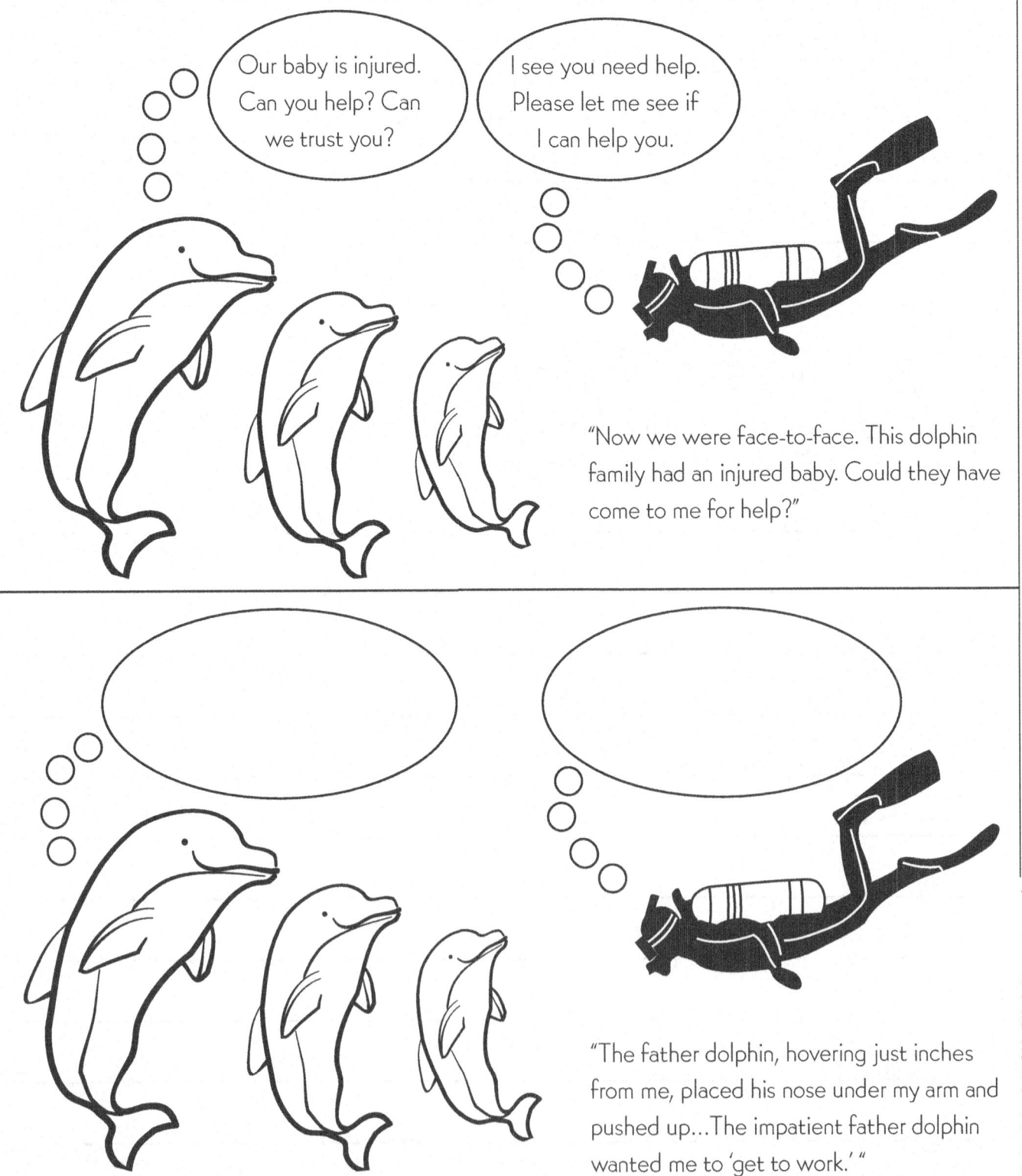

Dolphins: "Our baby is injured. Can you help? Can we trust you?"

Diver: "I see you need help. Please let me see if I can help you."

"Now we were face-to-face. This dolphin family had an injured baby. Could they have come to me for help?"

"The father dolphin, hovering just inches from me, placed his nose under my arm and pushed up...The impatient father dolphin wanted me to 'get to work.' "

Unit Five: Determination ~ (Textbook p. 428)

Name _____

Underwater Rescue

GRAPHIC ORGANIZER

Writing Dialogue

"I gently touched the hook shaft, and the baby made a high-pitched cry."

"Suddenly all three dolphins swam away, climbing toward the surface above. I had forgotten they had to breathe every few minutes."

Unit Five: Determination ~ (Textbook p. 428)

Underwater Rescue

GRAPHIC ORGANIZER
Writing Dialogue

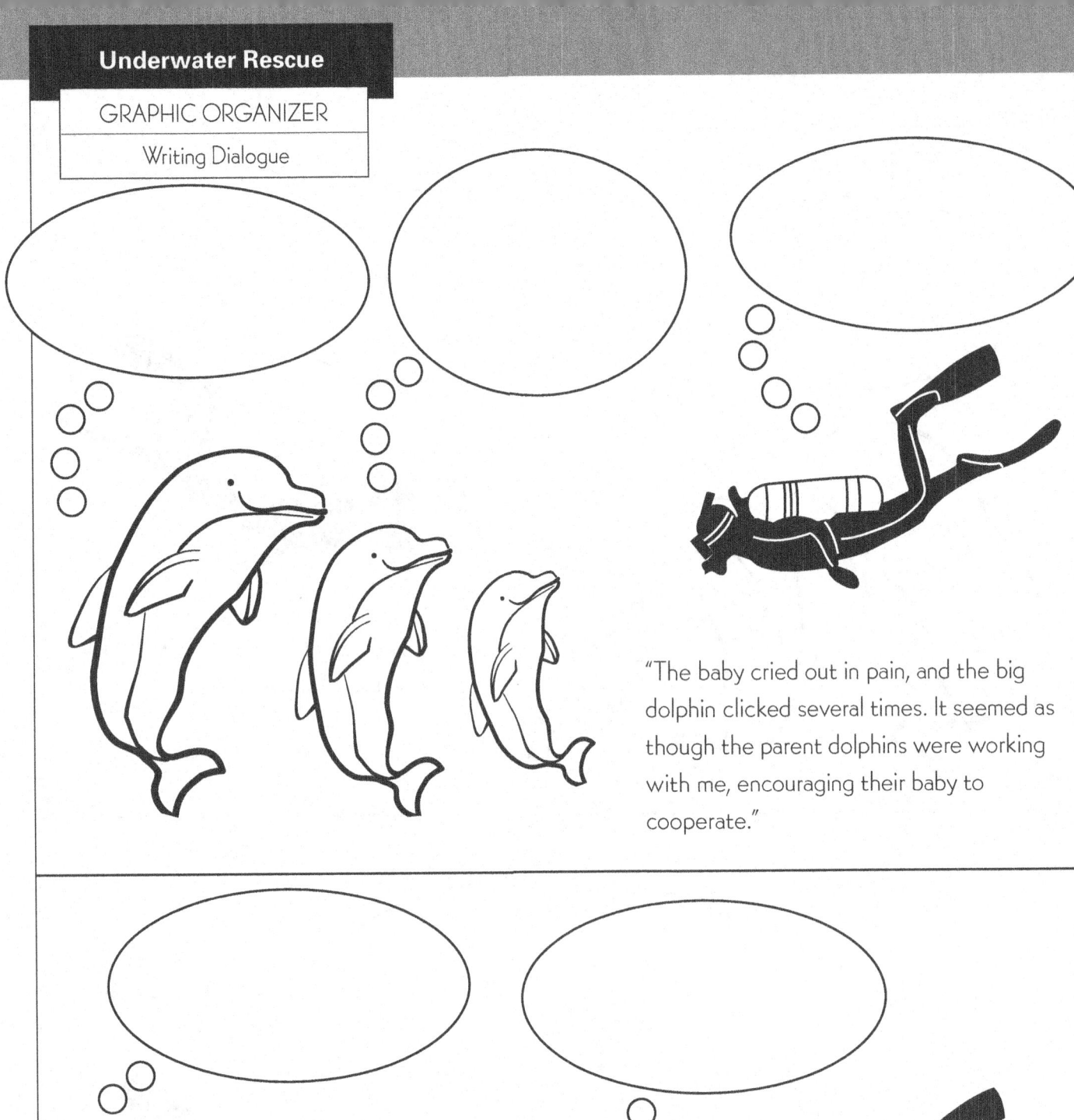

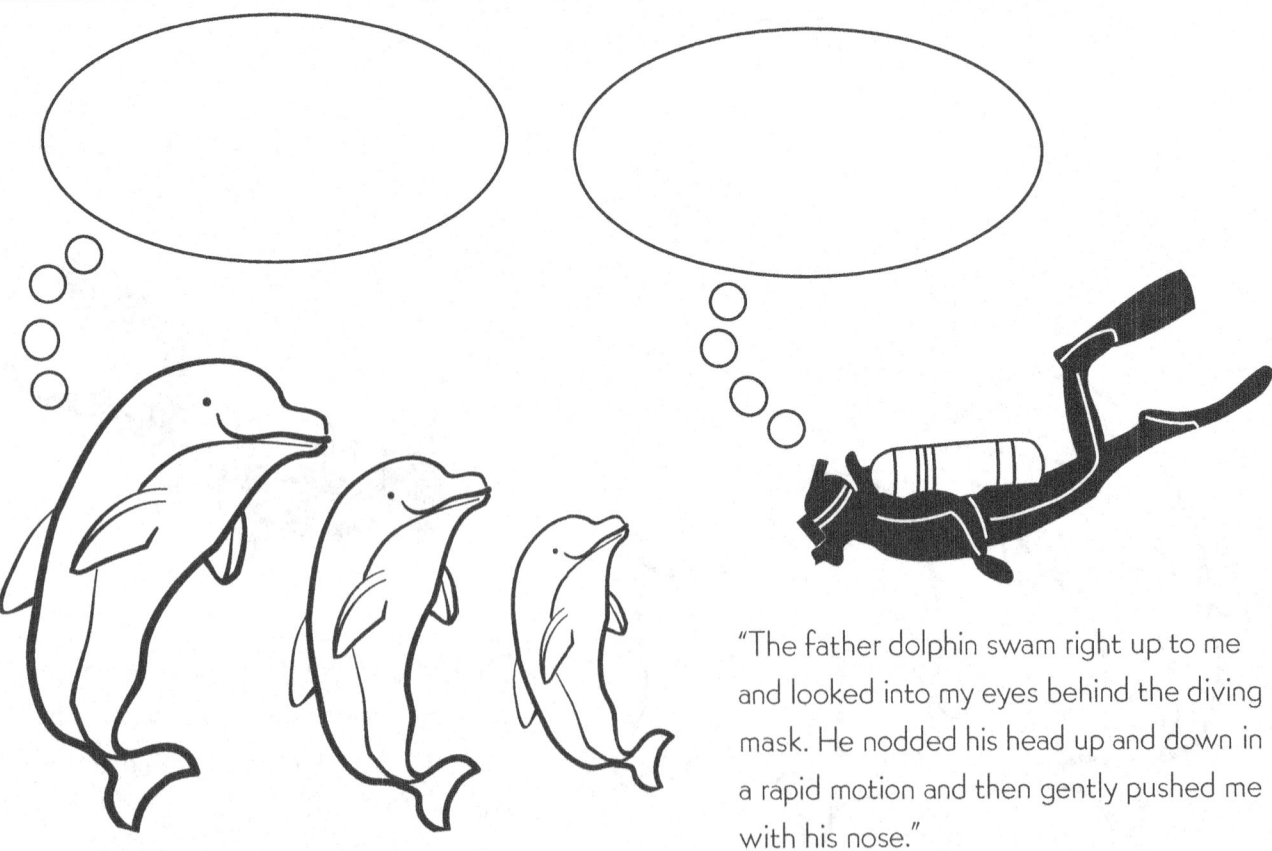

"The baby cried out in pain, and the big dolphin clicked several times. It seemed as though the parent dolphins were working with me, encouraging their baby to cooperate."

"The father dolphin swam right up to me and looked into my eyes behind the diving mask. He nodded his head up and down in a rapid motion and then gently pushed me with his nose."

Unit Five: *Determination* ~ (Textbook p. 428)

Name _____

Underwater Rescue

GRAPHIC ORGANIZER

Writing Dialogue

"Then I saw a small dolphin. It was in the midst of six other dolphins with a scar clearly visible on its back...It swam close to the boat...jumping high out of the water."

"I look forward to swimming with the dolphins again. It could happen anytime now."

Unit Five: *Determination* ~ (Textbook p. 428)   123

The Seven Children

COMPREHENSION Questions

In-Depth Thinking

1. Why do you think the map was given to the youngest child?

   _____
   _____
   _____
   _____

2. What do you think the farmer and his wife were doing while the children were in the woods?

   _____
   _____
   _____
   _____

3. Do you think the farmer and his wife were good parents? Why or why not?

   _____
   _____
   _____
   _____

Drawing Conclusions

4. The children had many faults but they did not ask their father for anything before he left the woods. What does this show?

   _____
   _____
   _____

Name _____

The Seven Children

COMPREHENSION
Questions

5. How long do you think it would have taken for the children to start working together if the youngest child had not screamed?

_____
_____
_____

6. The parents' solution to the children's behavior problem was a creative one, but it was a little bit risky. Can you think of some things that could have gone wrong?

_____
_____
_____

One Step Further

Even the weak become strong when they are united.
What do you think this means? Do you agree or disagree with this statement?

_____
_____
_____
_____
_____
_____
_____
_____

Unit Five: Determination ~ (Textbook p. 448)

The Seven Children

GRAPHIC ORGANIZER
Reviewing Subject Matter

When the children realized that they had been left in the woods, they fell into their usual bad habit of arguing and complaining. On the line provided under the pictures of the children, write what each of them said. If you have some extra time, you may color some details onto the drawings.

Unit Five: Determination ~ (Textbook p. 448)

Name _____

The Seven Children

GRAPHIC ORGANIZER

Reviewing Subject Matter

What had the parents put into each bundle? Write the answer into each of the bundles below. In the box at the bottom, write a short explanation of how the children were to use all the items in their bundles.

Unit Five: Determination ~ (Textbook p. 448)   127

The Garden of Happiness

COMPREHENSION Questions

In-Depth Thinking

1. Why do you think the adults chose to call the garden The Garden of Happiness?

2. How would you describe the "spirit" of the people in the neighborhood? Are they sad? Happy? Hopeful? Angry? See if you can express the way you think they felt about life in general. Base your answer on the story, not on how you think they *should* have felt.

3. What would Marisol's feelings have been at the end of the story had the teenagers not painted the beautiful mural?

Drawing Conclusions

4. Why is it important to tell us all of the adults' names and what they planted?

Unit Five: Determination ~ (Textbook p. 462)

Name _____

The Garden of Happiness

COMPREHENSION

Questions

5. What are some of Marisol's character traits?

_____

_____

_____

6. What life lesson can be learned from the advice of Mrs. Washington and Mrs. Rodriguez when Marisol's plant was dying?

_____

_____

_____

One Step Further

While there is life, there is hope. — Cicero

Do you know a story about someone who seemed to be in a hopeless situation and was suddenly saved from it? Share it with the class, because stories about hope make people hopeful. Hope is contagious!

Many books about people who never gave up hope are available today. If you know of a good one, share the name of it with your class.

_____

_____

_____

_____

_____

_____

Unit Five: *Determination* ~ (Textbook p. 462)

The Garden of Happiness

GRAPHIC ORGANIZER

Organizing with Graphics

The Garden of Happiness is about people. It tells of people from many countries who live together in New York.

The Garden of Happiness is about change. It starts in the springtime and ends in the late summer.

The Garden of Happiness is about hope. It starts in an empty lot full of rubbish and ends with a garden full of vegetables and flowers.

The author portrays a New York neighborhood, where many languages are spoken and people of many backgrounds live together. The author helps us get to know the neighborhood by using foreign-sounding names. Put the name of one character into each petal of the sunflower. If you know the character's nationality, write that in, too.

Characters

Name _____

The Garden of Happiness

GRAPHIC ORGANIZER

Organizing with Graphics

The story is full of foreign language words, just like those we would hear if we were to walk along East Houston Street. Write one foreign word or phrase into each petal of the sunflower. If you can, write its translation, too.

Foreign Words

Plants

What grew in The Garden of Happiness? Write the name of one plant or vegetable into each petal of the sunflower.

Unit Five: *Determination* ~ (Textbook p. 462)

One Grain of Rice

COMPREHENSION Questions

In-Depth Thinking

1. Why do you think the raja thought of himself as fair and wise?

   _____
   _____
   _____

2. How did the raja change between the beginning of the story and the end of the story?

   _____
   _____
   _____

3. Why was it wrong for the raja to make a feast during the famine?

   _____
   _____
   _____

Drawing Conclusions

4. To answer the following questions you must draw conclusions from statements made in the story. Answer each question by writing down the conclusion you have come to on that subject.

   a. How smart a man was the raja?

   _____

   b. Were the people generally satisfied to have the raja rule over them?

   _____

   c. Was the raja cruel?

Unit Five: Determination ~ (Textbook p. 482)

Name _____

One Grain of Rice
COMPREHENSION
Questions

5. How did Rani's idea show that she was a smart and caring person?

_____

_____

_____

6. What do you think would have happened to the people in the province had Rani not saved them?

_____

_____

_____

One Step Further

The power of numbers.
　　Think of an action, good or bad, that one person starts and then includes two other people. Each of the two people then includes two more people, each of those four include two more, and so on and on. For example, one person sneezes and two people catch colds.

_____

_____

_____

_____

_____

_____

_____

_____

Unit Five: Determination ~ (Textbook p. 482)

One Grain of Rice

GRAPHIC ORGANIZER

Looking Below the Surface

In *One Grain of Rice*, the reader keeps discovering that things are not "what they seem." In the exercise below, each phrase describes the way things appeared. Complete the sentence by writing what the real truth of the matter was.

Example: The raja believed he was wise and fair, but he was really...*very selfish, dishonest, and not at all good at math.*

1. The raja said he would save the rice for times of famine, but he really...
   _____
   _____
   _____

2. Each year the rice grew well and everyone should have had a lot, but...
   _____
   _____
   _____

3. The people asked the raja to give them some of the stored rice but...
   _____
   _____
   _____

4. Since it was the raja's land, he probably was hungry too, but really...
   _____
   _____
   _____

Unit Five: Determination ~ (Textbook p. 482)

Name _____

One Grain of Rice

GRAPHIC ORGANIZER

Looking Below the Surface

5. Rani looked as though she were stealing the rice, but really...
_____
_____
_____

6. Rani said she was asking for only a tiny reward, but really...
_____
_____
_____

7. After sixteen days, the raja noticed that he was giving Rani quite a lot of rice, but thought it wouldn't amount to much more, but really...
_____
_____
_____

8. If Rani had been like the raja, she would have kept all the rice for herself, but really... _____
_____
_____

9. The raja promised to take only as much rice as he needed from now on...
 AND HE REALLY DID!
_____
_____

Unit Five: Determination ~ (Textbook p. 482)

Maria's House

COMPREHENSION Questions

In-Depth Thinking

1. Clearly, Mama was a good mother. Describe some of the ways in which she served as a good role model for Maria.

   _____
   _____
   _____

2. Why didn't Maria talk to her mother about the assignment?

   _____
   _____
   _____

3. Contrast how Maria felt on the way to class with the way she felt at the end of the story.

   _____
   _____
   _____
   _____

Drawing Conclusions

4. Why did Maria throw her first assignment into the garbage instead of just putting the picture away?

   _____
   _____
   _____
   _____

Name _____

Maria's House

COMPREHENSION
Questions

5. What do you think about Mama's comment, "Art must be true"?

_____
_____
_____

6. What thoughts might Miss Lindstrom have had after Maria said, "But that *is* my house in the picture"?

_____
_____
_____

One Step Further

What matters is not what I think of him, but what he thinks of himself.
— Antoine De Saint Exupery

Explain the quote. Do you agree that what a person thinks of himself is more important than what others think of him? How concerned about other people's opinions should someone be? Is there such a thing as not being concerned enough? Is it possible to be *too* concerned?

_____
_____
_____
_____
_____
_____
_____
_____

Unit Five: Determination ~ (Textbook p. 500)

Maria's House

GRAPHIC ORGANIZER
Compare and Contrast

This story is called *Maria's House*, but it is really about several houses. Let us count them. There is Maria's house. Then there is the "magazine" house that Maria draws. There is the house that Jasper lives in. Finally, there is the house in which Jasper is *going* to live.

Each of the first four houses represents one of the four houses in the story. Write a small paragraph inside each house that answers at least three of the questions below. If you want to, you may decorate the house with crayons or markers. Decorate the last house the way you would want *your* house to look.

- Who lives in this house?

- What is one reason a person would want to live in this house?

- What is one reason a person would not want to live in this house?

- What are two details that make this house different from the others?

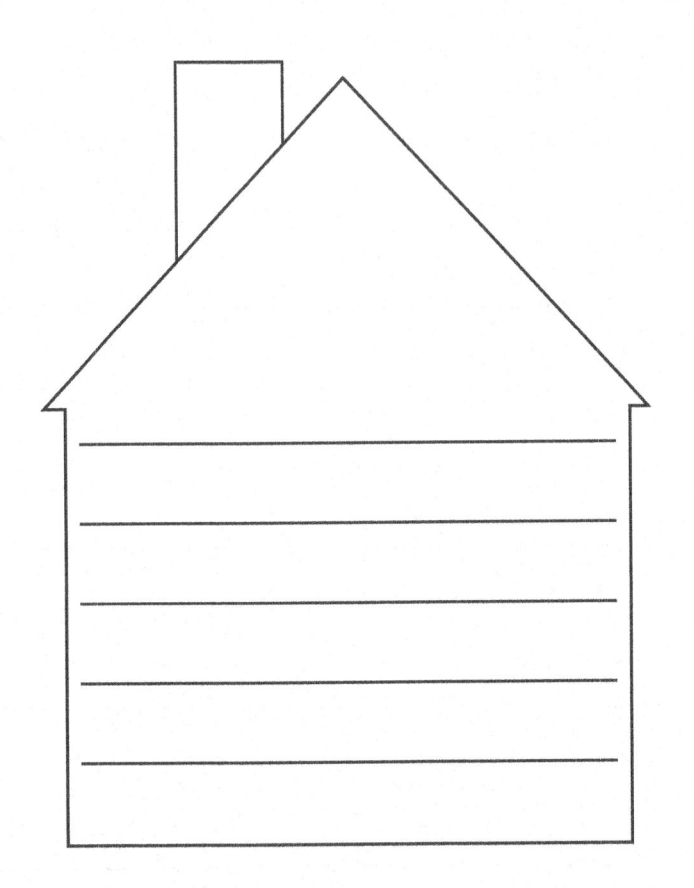

Unit Five: *Determination* ~ (Textbook p. 500)

Name _____

Maria's House
GRAPHIC ORGANIZER
Compare and Contrast

Unit Five: Determination ~ (Textbook p. 500)   139

The Bridge Dancers

VOCABULARY
Activity 1

| gorge | soaring | poultice | plunged | lulled |
| jubilant | quivery | pitching | thrashing | perilous |

1. Colorado! I had always wanted to see it, and here I was, walking next to a small stream in a deep _____ (*a small canyon through which a stream runs*).

2. Above me, the sky was a perfect blue, the color interrupted only by a large bird _____ (*flying high into the air*) high above us.

3. Suddenly, the stream took a sharp turn and the water _____ (*fell downward suddenly*) straight onto a pile of sharp rocks about a hundred yards below.

4. Only the alertness of our guide kept some of us from _____ (*falling sharply and suddenly*) forward over the cliff.

5. That close brush with death made me feel _____ (*shaky*) all over.

6. I began to realize that the blue sky and warm sun had _____ (*put to sleep by quiet, soothing means*) me into thinking that this would be a safe and easy hike.

7. Now I realized that the trail could be _____ (*dangerous*).

8. I began to imagine myself lying injured in the stream, the water _____ (*beating*) against me.

9. Next, my wild imagination pictured me being carried on a stretcher, a _____ (*a small moist bandage of cloth*) on my chest, and bandages on my arms and legs.

10. In the end, though, our trusty guide led us up out of the valley and all the way to the top of a hill, where we set up camp. A feeling of tremendous happiness filled me; my dream of hiking in Colorado was coming true—I was _____ (*full of joy*)!

Unit Six: The Grand Finalé ~ (Textbook p. 528)

Name _____

The Bridge Dancers

VOCABULARY

Activity II

Tongue Twisters

Can you write some tongue twisters using the vocabulary words provided? Don't forget, the tongue twisters have to make sense! Some of them have been done for you.

1. **quivery** *The quivery quail quarreled quietly, quickly quoting questions from quizzes.*

2. **pitches** (or pitch, pitched) _____

3. **thrashes** (or thrash, thrashed) _____

4. **herb** *Irv urged Irma to brew herbs in the urn.*

5. **soar** _____

6. **gorge** _____

7. **perilous** *Peter paid Paul to put Pat on the perilous plane to Paris, proudly planning to please Pat's Pa.*

8. **poultice** _____

9. **plunges** (or plunge, plunging) _____

10. **jubilant** *Jane, jubilant at winning genuine jewelry, joked about Jill's jealousy.*

Unit Six: The Grand Finalé ~ (Textbook p. 528)

The Bridge Dancers

COMPREHENSION Questions

In-Depth Thinking

1. Compare and contrast the two sisters, Callie and Maisie.

2. Maisie and Callie "speak" to one another with smiles, frightened eyes, and even yells of pain. They let each other know their thoughts without using words. Find an example of this on page 536 of the story.

3. Why doesn't Mama scold the girls for touching the ax?

Drawing Conclusions

4. List at least two phrases that help the reader picture the setting.

5. Why do you think the author chose the title, *The Bridge Dancers*?

Unit Six: The Grand Finalé ~ (Textbook p. 528)

Name _____

The Bridge Dancers

COMPREHENSION

Questions

6. Do you think that Maisie made the right decision to help Callie herself, and not wait for Mama to come?

_____
_____
_____

One Step Further

Whether you think you can or you can't—you are right. — Henry Ford

What did Henry Ford, the well-known founder of Ford Motor Company, mean by these words? How can a person be right either way? Does thinking you can do something really help you do it? Does thinking you can't do something prevent you from being able to do it?

_____
_____
_____
_____
_____
_____
_____
_____
_____
_____

Unit Six: The Grand Finalé ~ (Textbook p. 528)

The Bridge Dancers

GRAPHIC ORGANIZER
Sequencing

In *The Bridge Dancers* both sisters change. Maisie, however, changes a lot more than Callie does. She leaves behind some old personality traits and takes on new ones. At first, she is a timid girl who follows her sister's lead. Later, she turns into a strong girl who takes charge of a difficult situation. Below is a list of steps that Maisie took as she changed. Place them in the correct order into the sections of the bridge. The first one is done for you.

1. Maisie goes back to Callie and prepares a poultice and some feverfew tea.
2. Maisie objects to Callie's using the ax but doesn't really try to stop her.
3. Maisie steps onto the bridge with both feet.

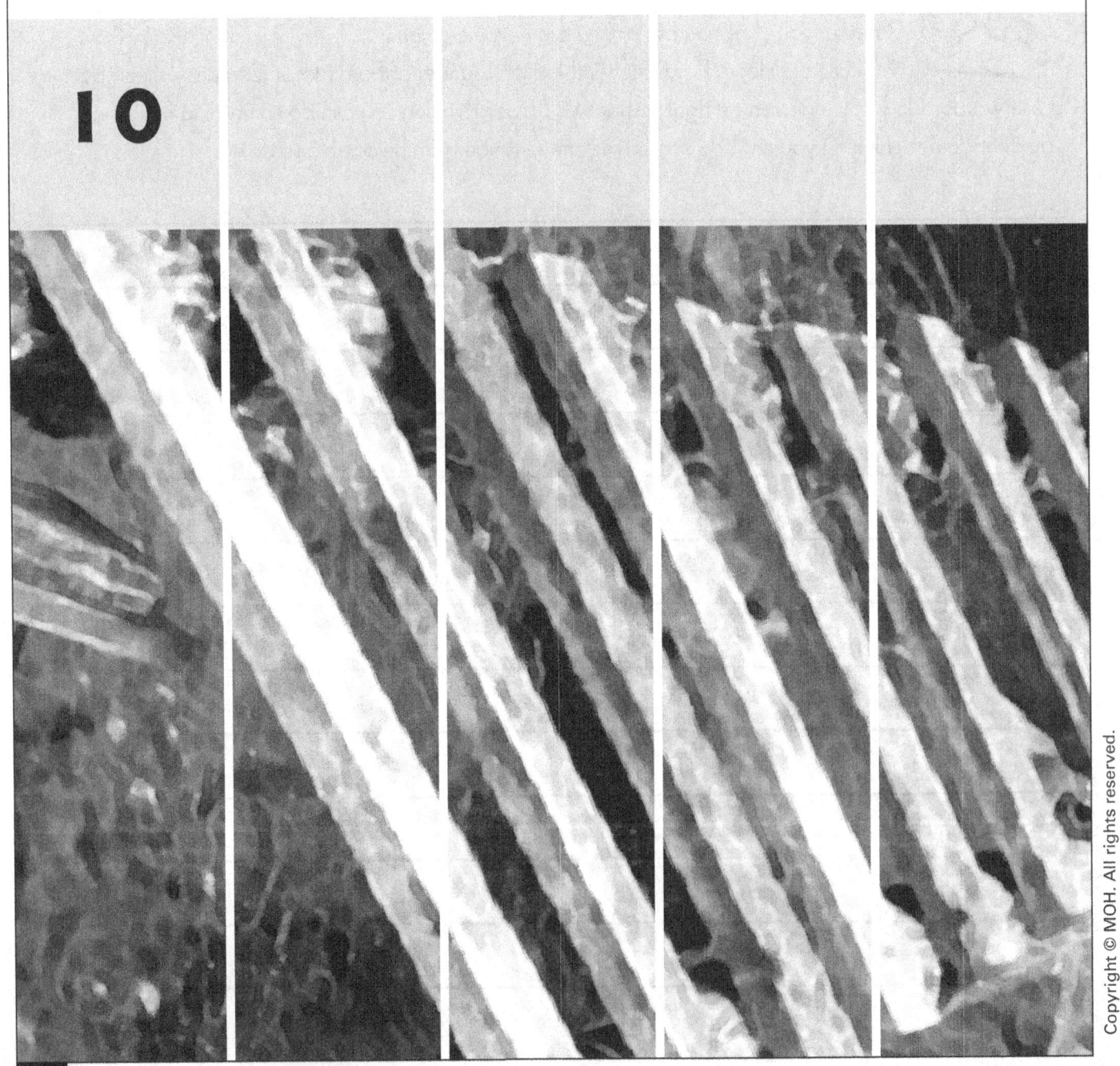

Unit Six: *The Grand Finale* ~ (Textbook p. 528)

Name _____

The Bridge Dancers

GRAPHIC ORGANIZER

Sequencing

4. Mama lets Maisie help her with her doctoring.
5. Maisie crawls back to the edge of the gorge, knowing she cannot cross the bridge.
6. Maisie stays up all night caring for Callie until Mama arrives.
7. Maisie is too frightened to go get Mama so she starts to doctor Callie herself.
8. Maisie is so afraid to cross the bridge in the storm that the fear stings her eyes.
9. Maisie is afraid for her mother to cross the bridge.
10. Maisie's heart jumps when Callie pretends to slip on the bridge.

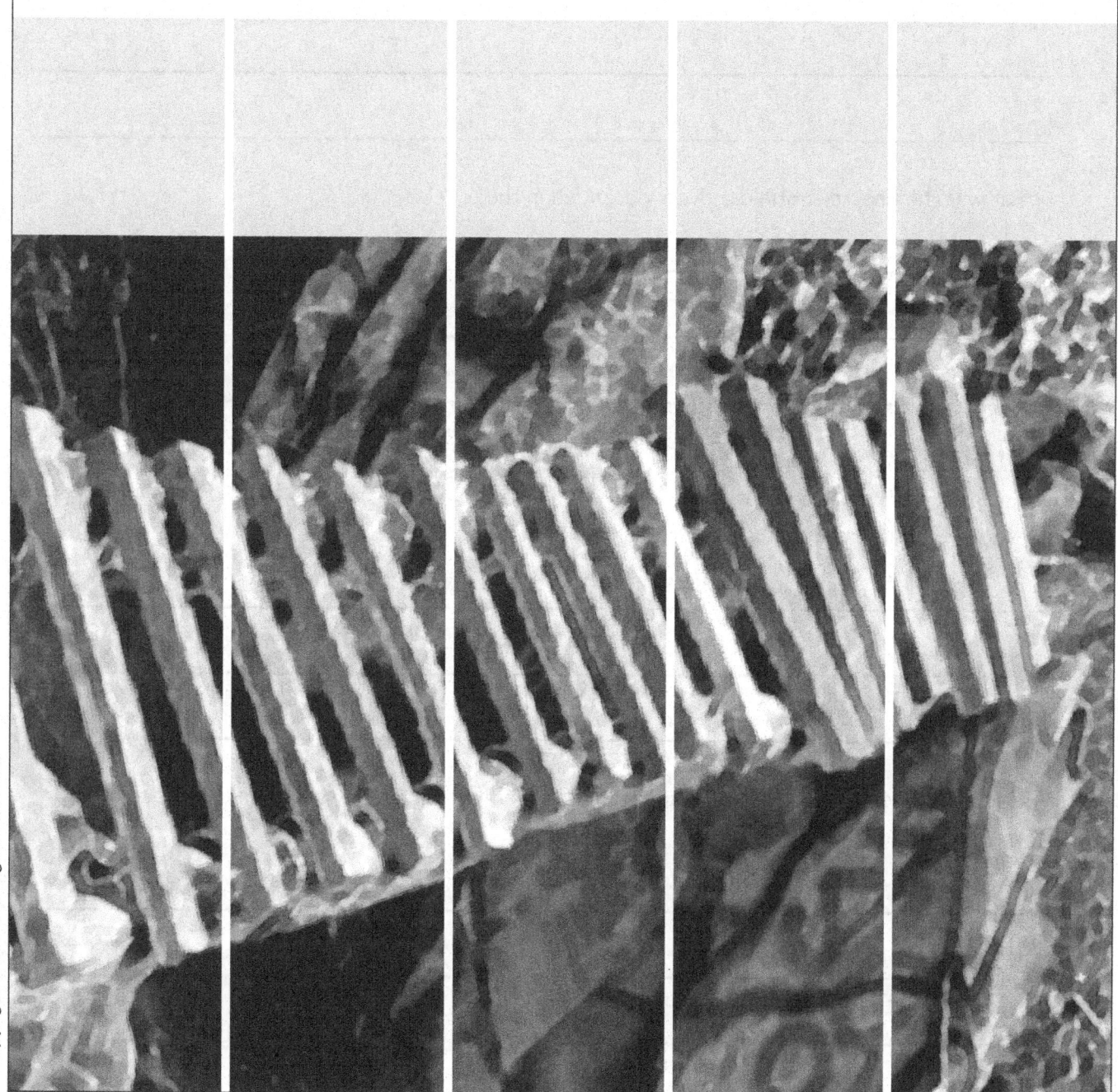

Unit Six: *The Grand Finalé* ~ (Textbook p. 528)

Dancing Bees

COMPREHENSION Questions

In-Depth Thinking

1. How do bees understand the waggle dance if the hive is dark?

   _____
   _____
   _____

2. What are a few things that the honeybee, with its tiny brain, can do very well?

   _____
   _____

3. What was the final scientific discovery described in the article?

   _____
   _____
   _____

Drawing Conclusions

4. How do you think the scientists planned and created their robotic bee?

   _____
   _____
   _____

5. What can you learn from the fact that Danish and German scientists worked on the experiment together?

   _____
   _____
   _____

Unit Six: The Grand Finalé ~ (Textbook p. 544)

Name _____

Dancing Bees

COMPREHENSION

Questions

6. Do you know of other scientific studies like this one? Describe what was studied and what was learned. If you don't know of any such study, suggest one that you think would be of interest to scientists, and describe how the study would be done.

One Step Further

Art gallery? Who needs it? Look up at the swirling silver-lined clouds in the magnificent blue sky or at the silently blazing stars at midnight. How could indoor art be any more masterfully created than G-d's museum of nature?
— Grey Livingston

Do you agree with this quote? Why or why not?

Unit Six: The Grand Finalé ~ (Textbook p. 544)   147

Dancing Bees

GRAPHIC ORGANIZER
Using Diagrams Effectively

It is often difficult for a reader to picture something described in words. This is why so many sets of instructions come with diagrams. In *Dancing Bees*, the author describes the dance of the bee that has found nectar. In the following exercise, we take you step by step with diagrams. Look at the list of quotations from the story on this page; they are not in order. Write each quotation under the diagram that it describes.

- "In a few minutes, the first bees to figure out where the food is fly away."
- "She repeats [the dance] over and over again as her sister bees watch."
- "When a honeybee discovers a rich supply of nectar, it flies back to the hive to tell the other bees exactly where the food is."
- "The most important part of the dance is the straight run through the middle of the figure eight."
- "The pattern of a bee's dance is a figure eight."
- "If the bee is dancing outside the hive on a flat surface, she lines up with the sun, then turns to point toward the food."

1.

2.

Unit Six: The Grand Finalé ~ (Textbook p. 544)

Name _____

Dancing Bees

GRAPHIC ORGANIZER
Using Diagrams Effectively

3.

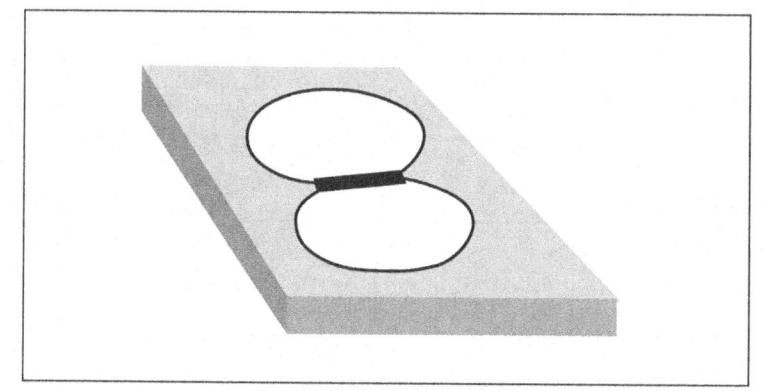

4.

5.

6.

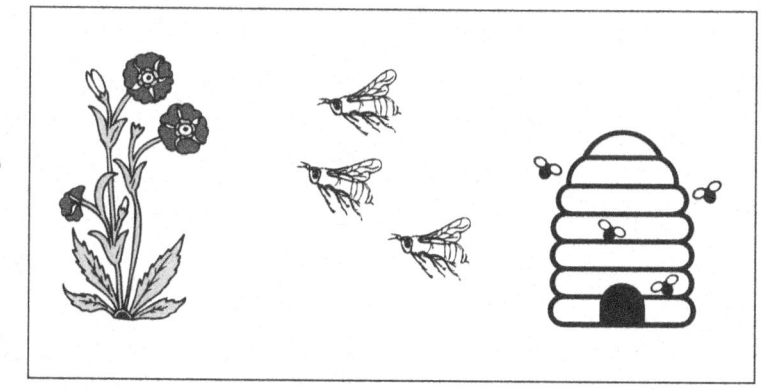

Unit Six: The Grand Finalé ~ (Textbook p. 544)   149

Name This American

VOCABULARY — Activity 1

| celebrities | doubt | inquisitive | monuments | podium |
| distinguished | indebted | misleading | observant | principal |

1. Our country has been blessed with many great and _____ (important and respected) leaders.

2. Many of them were modest men, with no desire to be famous _____ (well-known people).

3. George Washington, for example, rather than boasting of his own greatness, spoke about how _____ (owing; feeling obligated to repay something) he was to the soldiers who had fought to liberate America.

4. Abraham Lincoln, a humble man, had many _____ (a building or statue built in memory of a person or event) built to honor his memory.

5. It would be _____ (words or actions that lead people to believe something that is not true) to describe the life of a president as easy or enjoyable.

6. When we see a president speaking from the _____ (a small platform for a speaker) and being applauded, we think how wonderful it is to be famous.

7. Yet, one who is _____ (alert) will notice that most of a president's work is done in private.

8. He must work very hard and not question and _____ (to consider something unlikely) himself.

9. He must not allow himself to be annoyed by the many _____ (curious) people who disturb him constantly.

10. He must not be proud, even though he is the _____ (first in importance) speaker wherever he goes. His duty is to serve the country.

Unit Six: The Grand Finalé ~ (Textbook p. 552)

Name _____

Name This American
VOCABULARY
Activity II

Why or Why Not?

Answer the following questions.

1. Would **celebrities** be interesting to interview?
   Why or why not? <u>Yes, because most celebrities have interesting lives.</u>

2. Should you **doubt** what you read in the newspaper?
   Why or why not? _____

3. Do you feel **indebted** to your school?
   Why or why not? _____

4. Would an **observant** person make a good spy?
   Why or why not? _____

5. Would you want an **inquisitive** neighbor?
   Why or why not? _____

6. Do you think a school principal should be a **distinguished** person?
   Why or why not? _____

7. When you speak to the class, do you like to speak from a **podium**?
   Why or why not? _____

8. Is it **misleading** for a store to advertise an item at a low price and run out of the item on the first day of the sale?
   Why or why not? _____

9. Should the school's **principal** come along on all school trips?
   Why or why not? _____

10. Should **monuments** be built in honor of people who are living?
    Why or why not? _____

Unit Six: The Grand Finalé ~ (Textbook p. 552)

Name This American

COMPREHENSION Questions

In-Depth Thinking

1. List two things that you have learned that you did not know before reading this play.
   _____
   _____
   _____

2. Do you think the rules of the game show were fair?
   _____
   _____
   _____

3. In addition to a knowledge of American history, what skills would help a panelist guess the identity of the mystery guest?
   _____
   _____
   _____
   _____

Drawing Conclusions

4. Some of the panelists did not recognize the mystery guests even after they were told the guest's identity. Do you think the guest felt hurt or insulted? *Should* the guest have felt bad?
   _____
   _____
   _____
   _____

Unit Six: The Grand Finalé ~ (Textbook p. 552)

Name _____

Name This American

COMPREHENSION
Questions

5. Why do you think the playwright named the hosts Uncle Sam and Lady Liberty?

_____
_____
_____

6. List two important historical figures that you would add to this quiz game and explain why they should be included.

_____
_____
_____

One Step Further

You don't have to be a "person of influence" to be influential. The most influential people in your life are probably not even aware of the things they've taught you.

What is the difference between "a person of influence" and "an influential person"? Do you agree or disagree with the above opinion? Why or why not? How do people who are not famous influence you daily?

_____
_____
_____
_____
_____
_____
_____
_____

Unit Six: The Grand Finalé ~ (Textbook p. 552)

Name This American

GRAPHIC ORGANIZER
Process of Elimination

The panelists in *Name This American* had to discover the guest's identity by asking the guest questions. If the guest answered "yes" to a question, they knew they were on the right track. If the guest answered "no," that helped them, too, because they could then eliminate that possibility. Discovering the truth by eliminating all false answers is called **the process of elimination**.

Here is a simple example. An ice cream shop offers three flavors of ice cream: vanilla, chocolate, and strawberry. Your mother surprises you by telling you she has brought home some ice cream.

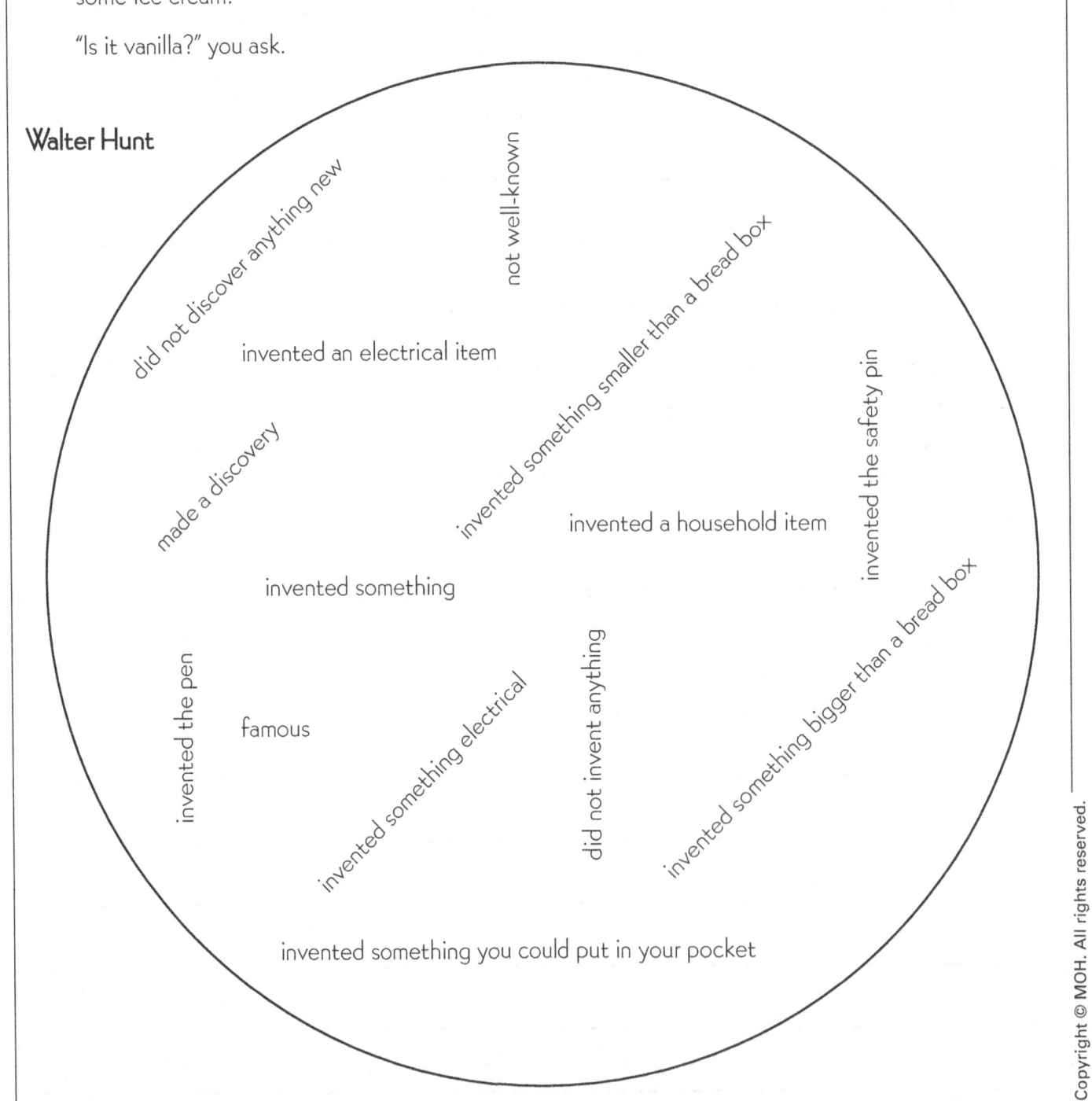

"Is it vanilla?" you ask.

Walter Hunt

(Inside circle:)
- did not discover anything new
- not well-known
- invented an electrical item
- invented something smaller than a bread box
- made a discovery
- invented the safety pin
- invented a household item
- invented something
- invented the pen
- invented something bigger than a bread box
- famous
- invented something electrical
- did not invent anything
- invented something you could put in your pocket

154 Unit Six: The Grand Finalé ~ (Textbook p. 552)

Name _____

Name This American

GRAPHIC ORGANIZER

Process of Elimination

"No."

"Is it strawberry?"

"No."

You don't have to ask any more questions. You know the ice cream has to be chocolate because you have **eliminated** the two other possibilities.

This exercise reviews the answers to the questions asked by the panelists. Draw a line through all the wrong answers. By eliminating them, you will be left with the right answers. Draw a circle around every answer that is true.

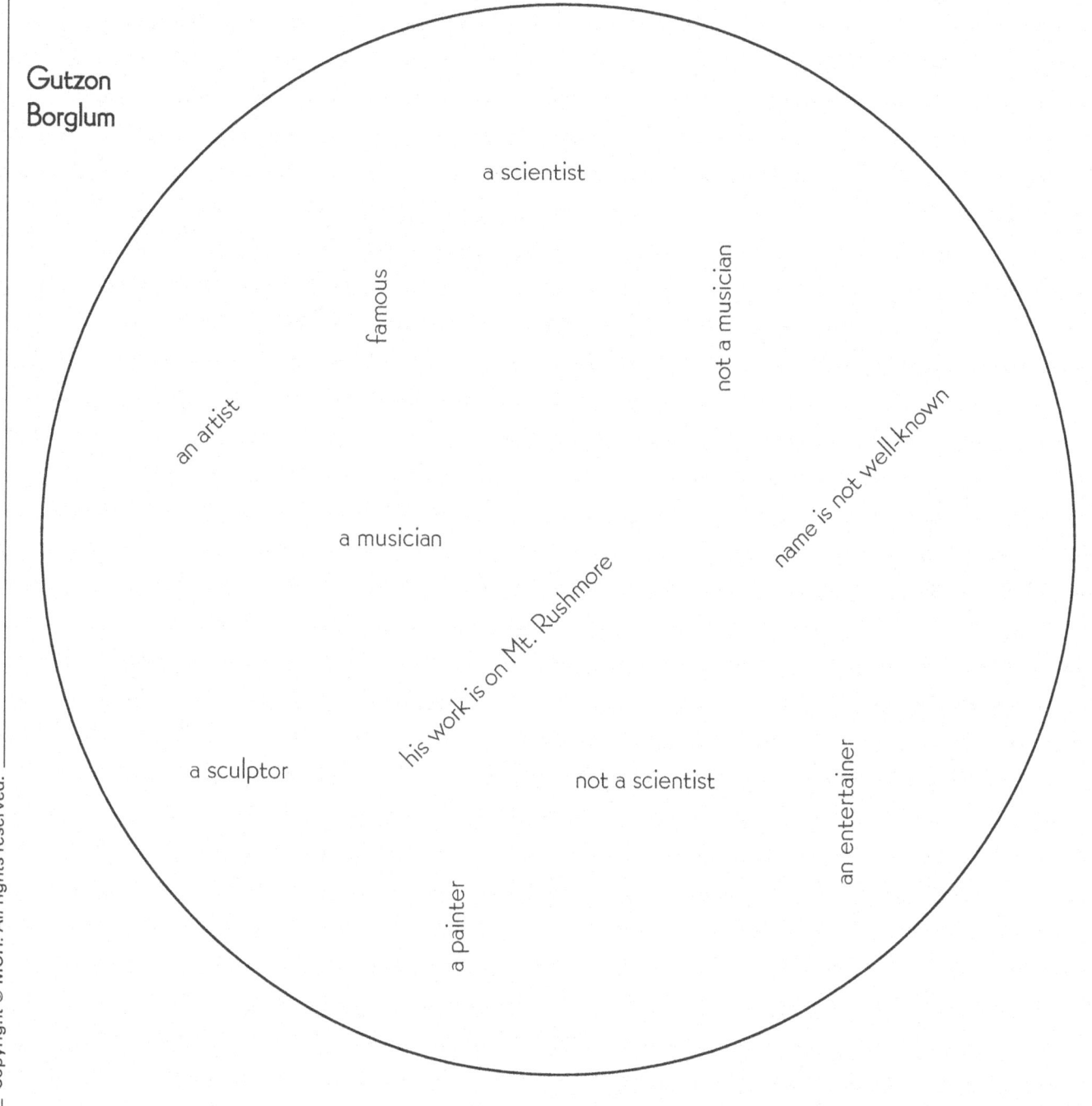

Gutzon Borglum

- a scientist
- famous
- not a musician
- an artist
- name is not well-known
- a musician
- his work is on Mt. Rushmore
- a sculptor
- not a scientist
- an entertainer
- a painter

Unit Six: *The Grand Finalé* ~ (Textbook p. 552)   155

Name This American

GRAPHIC ORGANIZER
Process of Elimination

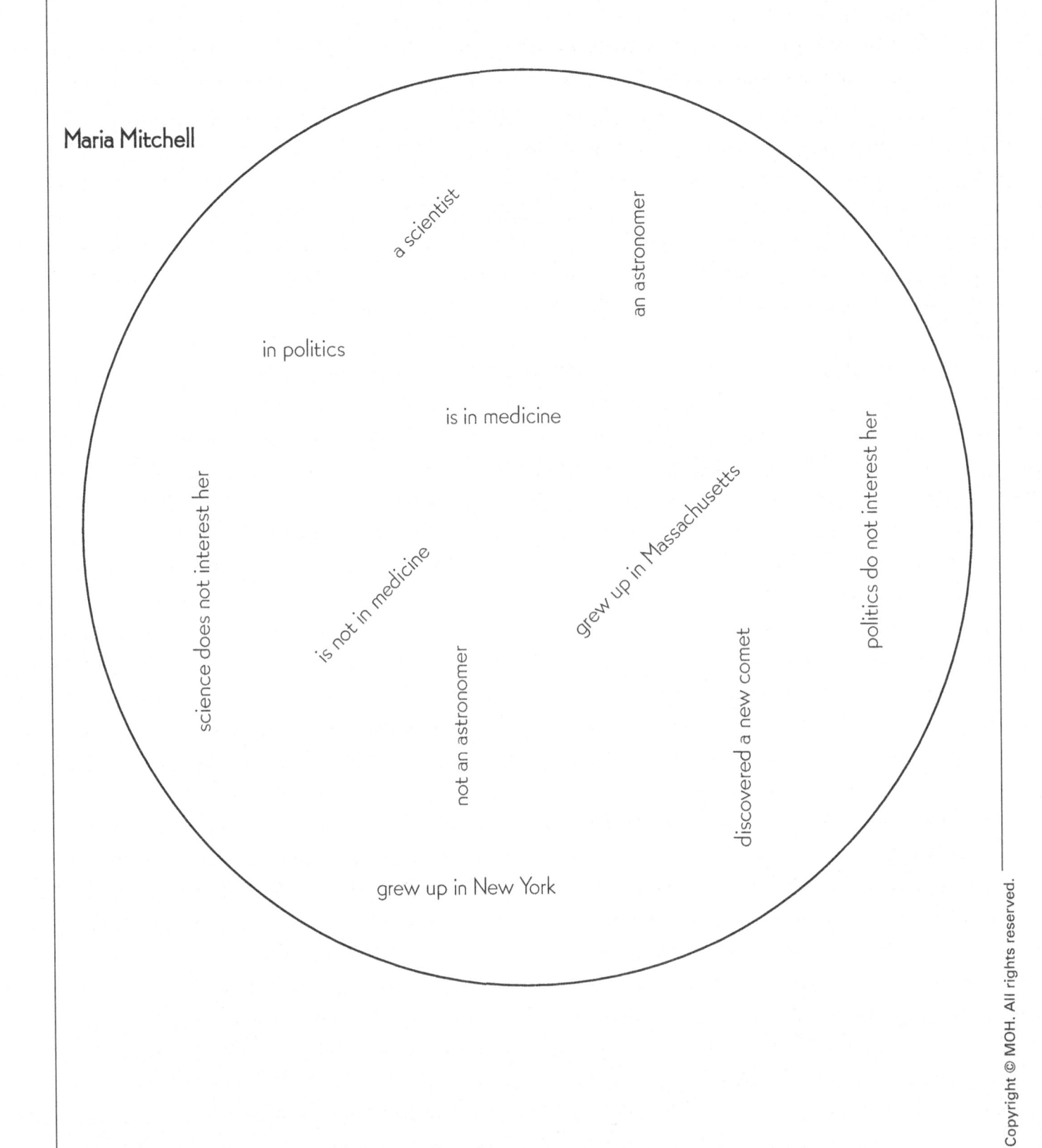

Maria Mitchell

- a scientist
- an astronomer
- in politics
- is in medicine
- science does not interest her
- is not in medicine
- grew up in Massachusetts
- politics do not interest her
- not an astronomer
- discovered a new comet
- grew up in New York

Unit Six: The Grand Finalé ~ (Textbook p. 552)

Name _____

Name This American

GRAPHIC ORGANIZER

Process of Elimination

Dolley Madison

- the wife of James Madison
- alive during the Revolutionary War
- living now
- was married to one of the first four presidents
- Mrs. Jefferson
- lived 200 years ago
- Martha Washington
- a seamstress who worked on the flag
- Mrs. Monroe
- Abigail Adams
- not alive during the Revolutionary War

Unit Six: The Grand Finalé ~ (Textbook p. 552)

Boss of the Plains

VOCABULARY
Activity 1

| bustling | distinctive | matted | picturesque | swig |
| crammed | huddled | pelts | saplings | technique |

1. Horace and Gilbert were British explorers. They went to South America in search of tribes whose clothing, language, and music were unusual and _____ (having a special style).

2. Before they left on their journey, they talked about the lovely, _____ (pleasing, interesting, and noticeable) villages they hoped to discover.

3. They planned to study the buildings and artwork of an unknown tribe, and hoped to copy their _____ (method) in art and other crafts.

4. As Horace and Gilbert trudged down a dirt path in the boiling sun, they noticed that someone had cut down _____ (young trees) to make a wider road.

5. Horace wiped his brow and took a _____ (mouthful of liquid) of water from his canteen.

6. "Do you think we are near a village?" he asked Gilbert. "This area is not exactly busy and _____ (full of activity); as a matter of fact, I haven't heard a sound in hours."

7. "You have a point, Horace," said Gilbert. "This land is not what you would call _____ (crowded; stuffed) with lots of people."

8. As they walked on, they saw a few huts. On the ground, a few men were sitting _____ (gathered closely together) around a large tub.

9. "Hello there," said Horace, cheerily. "What are you all doing?" The two explorers saw a pile of animal _____ (animal skins that have not been prepared for use) stacked up next to the tub.

10. "They seem to be tanning hides," said Gilbert to Horace. He bent down and patted one of the pelts. "Just look at how thick and _____ (tangled) the fur on that hide is!" No sooner had he touched the pile of furs than the entire group of men leaped up and started shouting at the two explorers. "We had better run," said Gilbert, "before they tan *our* hides!"

Unit Six: The Grand Finale ~ (Textbook p. 570)

Name _____

Boss of the Plains

VOCABULARY

Activity II

Opposites Attract!

Draw a line between the vocabulary word and its opposite.

1. bustling   ordinary

2. crammed   ugly

3. distinctive   empty

4. huddled   old tree

5. matted   slow-paced

6. picturesque   spaced far apart

7. sapling   combed out

Write a sentence with the remaining three words.

1. pelts _____
   _____

2. swig _____
   _____

3. technique _____
   _____

Unit Six: The Grand Finalé ~ (Textbook p. 570)

Boss of the Plains

COMPREHENSION Questions

In-Depth Thinking

1. John Stetson, like so many others, dreamed of going out West to strike it rich. Which part of his dream was fulfilled and which part was not?

   _____
   _____
   _____

2. "But he still had a trade and a talent." (page 577) Why are these words so important to the story?

   _____
   _____
   _____

3. What actually made the Stetson hat, known as the Boss of the Plains, so famous?

   _____
   _____

Drawing Conclusions

4. How do you think John Stetson's father in New Jersey would have felt about his son's success?

   _____
   _____

5. What were some good business ideas that John had?

   _____
   _____
   _____

Unit Six: The Grand Finalé ~ (Textbook p. 570)

Name _____

Boss of the Plains

COMPREHENSION

Questions

6. When the horseman paid John five dollars for his hat, what did John suddenly realize?

_____

_____

_____

One Step Further

When a person needs something, the need forces the person to find a way to solve the problem. The result is often a new invention.

Write about some inventions that came about because somebody needed to find a solution for a particular problem.

_____

_____

_____

_____

_____

_____

_____

_____

_____

_____

_____

_____

Unit Six: The Grand Finalé ~ (Textbook p. 570) 161

Boss of the Plains

GRAPHIC ORGANIZER
Reviewing

Like so many people in United States history, John Stetson had to go west to find success. And, like so many people in the history of the entire world, John Stetson experienced failure and disappointment before he achieved success. On the map below, trace John Stetson's travels by drawing a line between each of the places in which he lived.

Start at

1. Orange, New Jersey, and draw a line to
2. St. Joseph, Missouri. From St. Joseph, draw a line to
3. Pike's Peak in Colorado. Draw a line from there to
4. Philadelphia, Pennsylvania.

After that, draw a dotted line back to Pike's Peak to show where John's hats were shipped and sold.

Unit Six: The Grand Finalé ~ (Textbook p. 570)

Name _____

Boss of the Plains

GRAPHIC ORGANIZER

Reviewing

How do you make felt?

First, take a _____.
In the middle of it, pile _____ _____.
Next, make an _____ _____ and flick it over the fur.
Take a swig of _____ and _____ it over the fur.
Take the matted fur and dip it in _____ _____.
You now have FELT!

What are six things that Stetsons are good for? Write an answer in each hat.

1 2 3 4 5 6

Unit Six: *The Grand Finalé* ~ (Textbook p. 570)

Stone Fox

VOCABULARY — Activity 1

stunned	treacherous	abruptly	clenched	frigid
amateur	jagged	abreast	effortlessly	overtake

1. Hans had grown up in the Alps Mountains in Switzerland. Although he had skied all his life, he was not a professional skier; he was still an _____ (beginner lacking in skill).

2. Hans and his friends had formed a skiing club long ago. Each weekend, they would meet to climb a difficult and _____ (very dangerous) mountain.

3. They were never discouraged by the _____ (freezing) weather; they liked the cold.

4. They would hike up the mountain two or three _____ (side by side).

5. When they reached a certain point, they would get ready to race down, each one trying to _____ (come from behind and then pass) whoever was in the lead.

6. Today was no different. The boys in the group were racing down the mountain, when Hans noticed that William, who had taken the lead, had stopped _____ (suddenly).

7. Hans was _____ (shocked). Something terrible must have happened.

8. The other boys saw Hans and William from afar and were able to slow down with ease, almost _____ (easily). "What happened?" they demanded.

9. William stood there with his fists _____ (held closed tightly) in anger. He was furious.

10. "Someone has pushed a _____ (rough, sharp, and uneven) boulder right into our path. If I hadn't stopped suddenly, some of you could have run right into it and been badly hurt." All of us stood there silently for a moment, then we pounded him on the back, cheered him, and thanked him over and over.

Stone Fox

VOCABULARY

Activity II

Name _____

Tug of War!

Do you know a pair of friends who do nothing but argue? One says it's cold; the other says it's hot! One says it's old; the other says it's not! Every conversation is a tug of war!

In the exercise below, you will find a statement or comment in a box on the left. In the box on the right, write a sentence that is the opposite of the friend's comment, using the vocabulary word provided.

1. "I wasn't the least bit surprised that they chose Tom as captain of the football team."	"Are you kidding? I was **stunned** that a guy who can't throw, run, or tackle was chosen."
2. "Those basketball players look really professional." **[amateur]**	
3. "Let's take that path; it looks pretty safe." **[treacherous]**	
4. "I don't think you need to worry when you pass that boulder; it has a smooth surface." **[jagged]**	
5. "He seemed awfully relaxed; he talked and joked and finally walked out of the office." **[abrupt]**	
6. "If I remember correctly, we walked down that hill single-file." **[abreast]**	
7. "I'm sure he wasn't angry. He looked calm and spoke quietly." **[clenched]**	
8. "Don't ask her to play the piano at our party; it will be too much work for her to prepare something to play." **[effortlessly]**	
9. "Tell Mike to jump in the pool; the water's warm!" **[frigid]**	
10. "We are going to win this race—they will never catch us now!" **[overtake]**	

Unit Six: The Grand Finalé ~ (Textbook p. 586)

Stone Fox

COMPREHENSION Questions

In-Depth Thinking

1. What are some similarities and differences between Willy and Stone Fox?

　

2. How were the ways in which Willy and Stone Fox raced different from one another?

　

3. Why do you think Grandfather had the strength to watch Willy as he raced by his window?

　

Drawing Conclusions

4. Why didn't anyone else in the crowd step forward to assist Willy?

　

5. How would you have reacted if Stone Fox hit you? Why do you think that Willy continued to be friendly to Stone Fox even after Stone Fox hit him?

Unit Six: The Grand Finalé ~ (Textbook p. 586)

Name _____

Stone Fox

COMPREHENSION

Questions

6. Did Willy really deserve to win the race?

_____
_____
_____
_____

One Step Further

Where there is a will, there is a way.

What is the meaning of this saying? Do you agree or disagree with this statement? Support your answer.

_____
_____
_____
_____
_____
_____
_____
_____
_____
_____
_____

Unit Six: The Grand Finalé ~ (Textbook p. 586)

Stone Fox

GRAPHIC ORGANIZER
Outlining the Plot

Stone Fox has so much action that it may be difficult to remember every part of the plot. To help you, we have designed a game called "captions." These are the instructions: each picture hints at one part of the plot. The pictures are in order. The twelve sentences on this page are not in order. Find the sentence that describes each picture and write its letter on the line under the picture. When you are done, you will have an outline of the story.

CAPTIONS

a. His eye is swollen and sore.
b. Willy and Searchlight are the winners.
c. Willy goes to Lester the pharmacist and gets the medicine.
d. After a while, Stone Fox catches up and takes the lead.
e. The gun goes off and the race begins.
f. Doc Smith gives Willy a prescription and a piece of cake.
g. Inside he finds the five Samoyeds.
h. Searchlight collapses just as they approach the finish line. Willy carries him over the finish line.
i. The night before the race, Willy goes to the doctor to get medicine for his grandfather.
j. Stone Fox comes up and slaps him.
k. On his way home he passes an old barn.
l. Willy and Searchlight take the lead.

Name _____

Stone Fox

GRAPHIC ORGANIZER
Outlining the Plot

1. _____

2. _____

3. _____

4. _____

5. _____

6. _____

7. _____

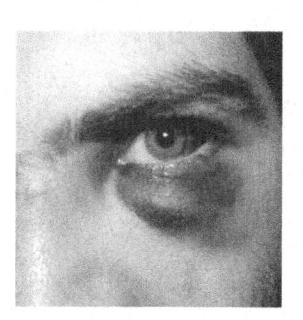

8. _____

9. _____

10. _____

11. _____

12. _____

Unit Six: The Grand Finalé ~ (Textbook p. 586)   169

Glossary

A

abreast (uh BREST) *adv., adj.*: side by side

abrupt (uh BRUPT) *adj.*: sudden

absurd (ub ZURD) *adj.*: ridiculous

abundantly (uh BUN dunt lee) *adv.*: very much

affected (uh FEK tid) *v.*: influenced

agonized (AG uh NYZD) *v.*: worried unhappily

agriculture (AG rih kull chur) *n.*: farming [related word]

allotment (uh LOT ment) *n.*: the portion of something that is assigned to someone

amateurs (AM uh churz) *n.*: beginners lacking in skill and experience; not experts

anticipation (an TISS ih PAY shun) *n.*: happily looking forward to something

appointment *n.*: position; job

apprentice (uh PREN tiss) *n.*: a person who works for another in order to learn a trade

auctioneer (AWK shuh NEER) *n.*: the person who conducts the auction [related word]

B

balmy (BAH mee) *adj.*: mild and refreshing weather

basking (BASS king) *v.*: lying in something pleasantly warm (like the sun)

battered (BAT erd) *adj.*: damaged by rough and careless treatment

beacon (BEE kun) *n.*: a light used as a warning signal

bolt *v.*: suddenly run away

brandishing (BRAN dish ing) *v.*: waving and displaying

budge (BUHJ) *v.*: move even slightly

bustling (BUSS ling) *v.*: full of activity

C

calico (KAL ih ko) *n.*: a plain cotton fabric printed on one side

cataloging (CAT uh LOG ing) *v.*: organizing a list of items into groups

celebrities (suh LEB rih teez) *n.*: well-known or famous people

chiseled (TCHIH zuld) *v.*: carved with a *chisel*, a tool with a cutting edge designed to carve a hard material

chores (TSHORZ) *n.*: the everyday work around a house or farm; a small job that must be done regularly

churned *v.*: shook and beat milk to turn it into butter

chute (SHOOT) *n.*: a narrow, sloping passageway for delivering items from a higher to a lower level

clenched (KLENSHT) *v.*: held closed tightly

Glossary

club (KLUB) *n.*: a heavy stick

clutched (KLUCHD) *v.*: held onto tightly

cobblestone (KOB ul stone) *n.*: a small, naturally rounded stone, used in paving roads, before asphalt became popular

collateral (kuh LAT uh rull) *n.*: property promised as guarantee for a loan [related word]

commercial (kuh MUR shul) *n.*: made by companies to be sold in stores; not homemade

commotion (kuh MO shun) *n.*: noise and disturbance

competently (KAHM puh tunt lee) *adv.*: doing something in a good, but not outstanding way [related word]

composed (kum POZED) *v.*: made up of

confined (kun FYND) *v.*: restricted; kept from leaving a place

console (kun SOLE) *v.*: comfort

consternation (KAHN stur NAY shun) *n.*: a sudden alarming amazement or dread

consulting (kun SULT ing) *v.*: asking advice of

contestants (kun TEST unts) *n.*: people who take part in a competition [related word]

contracts (KAHN trakts) *n.*: written agreements between two parties [related word]

corroded (kuh RODE id) *adj.*: worn away

crammed (KRAMD) *v.*: crowded; stuffed

craned (KRAYND) *v.*: stretched out their necks (to see)

crest *n.*: the highest part of a hill

crude *adj.*: rough; not well-designed

cultivate (KUL tih vayt) *v.*: to help the plants grow by tending to the soil around them

D

debt (DETT) *n.*: something that is owed [related word]

debris (duh BREE) *n.*: the remains of anything destroyed

decreed (dih KREED) *v.*: ordered; commanded

delegate (DELL uh gut) *n.*: one person sent by a group of people to represent them at a convention

dense (DENSS) *adj.*: thick and tightly packed together

desolately (DESS uh lit lee) *adv.*: very sadly

devastation (DEH vis TAY shun) *n.*: destruction and ruin

devour (dih VOW ehr) *v.*: to swallow hungrily

distinctive (dis TINK tiv) *adj.*: unusual; having a special style

distinguished (dis TEENG wishd) *v.*: important and respected

domain (doe MAYN) *n.*: a region inhabited by a certain type of wildlife

donned (DAHND) *v.*: put on

Glossary

doubt (DOWT) *v.*: to consider something unlikely [related word]

doused (DOWST) *v.*: threw water on

drought (DROWT) *n.*: a long period of dry weather [related word]

dwarfed (DWORFD) *v.*: appeared small by comparison

E

eaves (EEVZ) *n.*: the overhanging lower edges of a roof

eerie (IH ree) *adj.*: strange and somewhat frightening

efficiently (ih FISH unt lee) *adv.*: doing something with little or no waste of time and effort [related word]

effortlessly (EFF urt less lee) *adv.*: easily

embedded (em BED ed) *v.*: set deeply into

engrossed (en GROSED) *v.*: occupied; completely involved in

enraged (en RAYJD) *adj.*: extremely angry

evaporating (ee VAP uh RAY ting) *v.*: disappearing

executive (egg ZEK yoo tiv) *n.*: a person who has a position of leadership in a business or company

expedition (EX puh DISH un) *n.*: a journey or voyage made to a distant place for a certain purpose

F

famine (FAM in) *n.*: a hunger; a major food shortage

financial (fy NAN shul) *adj.*: relating to money matters [related word]

flaw *n.*: a defect; an imperfection

flint stones *n.*: hard stones used to produce a spark

frigid (FRIH jud) *adj.*: freezing [related word]

G

gingerly (JIN jur lee) *adv.*: with great care

glistened (GLISS und) *v.*: shone

gorge (GORJ) *n.*: a small canyon through which a stream runs

grim *adj.*: serious and unpleasant

grippe (GRIP) *n.*: influenza

gullies (GULL eez) *n.*: small valleys or ravines made by running water

H

habitat (HAB ih TAT) *n.*: the place where a plant or animal is naturally found

haltingly (HALT ing lee) *adv.*: slowly, with hesitation

haughty (HAW tee) *adj.*: snobbish; arrogant

hearth (HARTH) *n.*: the floor of a fireplace

Glossary

herded (HURD id) *v.*: drove or led (cows)

hoisted (HOYS tid) *v.*: raised

horizon (huh RY zun) *n.*: the place in the distance where the earth and sky seem to meet

hovered (HUV urd) *v.*: waited nearby

huddled (HUH dld) *v.*: gathered closely together

I

impact (IM pakt) *n.*: the force with which one thing hits another

implored (im PLORD) *v.*: begged

income (INK um) *n.*: the money an individual or business makes during a given time period

indebted (in DET ed) *adj.*: owing; obligated to repay something

inquisitive (in KWIZ uh tiv) *adj.*: curious [related word]

inspired (in SPY ehrd) *v.*: filled with a sense of purpose

instinctively (in STINK tiv lee) *adv.*: without thinking; from an inborn knowledge, not as a result of having been taught

interchangeable (IN tur CHAYNGE uh bul) *adj.*: two things that can be used in place of one another

inundated (IN un DAY tud) *v.*: flooded

J

jagged (JAG ud) *adj.*: rough, sharp, and uneven

jarring (JAR ing) *v.*: shaking

jauntily (JAWNT ih lee) *adv.*: in a lively, carefree, and slightly proud way

jubilant (JOO bih lunt) *adj.*: full of joy

K

kindling (KIHND ling) *n.*: material that ignites easily, used to start a fire

L

linger (LEENG er) *v.*: to stay somewhere longer than necessary because one does not want to leave

lull *n.*: a temporary calm

lulling (LULL ing) *v.*: putting to sleep by quiet, soothing means

luminous (LOO mih nuss) *adj.*: reflecting light

M

magistrate (MADJ iss trayt) *n.*: a government worker who enforces the law

maneuvered (muh NOO vurd) *v.*: moved about and changed direction as required

manipulate (muh NIP yoo layt) *v.*: handle with skill

matted (MAT ed) *adj.*: thick and tangled

Glossary

meandered (mee AN derd) *v.*: wound around gently from one place to another

menacing (MEN uh sing) *adj.*: threatening

miscalculated (mis KAL kyuh LAY tid) *v.*: judged incorrectly

misleading (miss LEED ing) *adj.*: words or actions that lead people to believe something that is not true

mock *adj.*: pretend; make believe

monologue (MAH nuh log) *n.*: a long speech made by one person, with no answer or interruption from the listener

monument (MAHN yoo munt) *n.*: a building, statue, or the like, built in memory of a person or event

mural (MYOOR ul) *n.*: a large picture painted directly on a wall or ceiling

mustering (MUST uh ring) *v.*: gathering; calling upon

N

needlessly (NEED luss lee) *adv.*: unnecessarily

O

observant (ub ZUR vunt) *adj.*: alert [related word]

ominous (AH mih nuss) *adj.*: threatening; hinting that something bad is about to happen

orb (ORB) *n.*: a round object [related word]

ornery (OR nuh ree) *adj.*: mean

overtake (O ver TAYK) *v.*: come from behind and then pass [related word]

P

parable (PAIR uh bul) *n.*: a short story designed to teach a true or moral lesson [related word]

parchment (PARCH ment) *n.*: a stiff, heavy, ivory-colored paper made from the skins of sheep or goats

pare (PAIR) *v.*: to cut off the outer layer

passion (PASH un) *n.*: an enthusiasm for something

peer *n.*: one who is the equal of another

pelts *n.*: animal skins that have not been prepared for use in clothing or other items

perilous (PEH ruh luss) *adj.*: dangerous [related word]

persimmon (pur SIH mun) *n.*: a large, plumlike orange fruit that is sweet when very ripe

picturesque (PIK chur ESK) *adj.*: pleasing, interesting, and noticeable

pirouettes (PEER oo ETS) *n.*: a dance step in which the dancer whirls about on one foot

pitch *n.*: a black, sticky tar

pitches *v.*: falls sharply

plain *n.*: a large flat area of land

plucked (PLUKD) *v.*: pulled out, like feathers from a bird

plunges (PLUNJ iz) *v.*: falls down suddenly

poacher (POE chur) *n.*: a person who hunts or fishes in an area where it is illegal for him or her to do so

podium (PO dee um) *n.*: a small platform for a speaker, orchestra conductor, or the like
portfolio (port FO lee o) *n.*: a flat, portable case for carrying loose papers, drawings, and the like
poultice (POLE tiss) *n.*: a small moist bandage of cloth or herbs
precision (prih SIZH un) *n.*: being exact about every detail
predator (PREH duh tor) *n.*: an animal that hunts other animals for food
principal (PRIN sih pul) *adj.*: first in importance
propelled (pruh PELD) *v.*: moved; driven
proposal (pruh PO zul) *n.*: a suggested plan
pungent (PUN junt) *adj.*: sharp and strong (used only to describe a taste or smell)

Q

quibbled (KWIH buld) *v.*: argued about some small, unimportant detail
quivered (KWIV erd) *v.*: shook slightly
quivery (KWIH vuh ree) *adj.*: shaky

R

raja (RAH zha) *n.*: the title of a chieftain or prince in India and areas of southeast Asia
realign (REE uh LYN) *v.*: to return to the proper position
reef *n.*: a ridge of rocks or sand near the surface of the water
rehabilitation (REE huh BIH luh TAY shun) *n.*: a regaining of health and strength
relinquish (rih LINK wish) *v.*: let go of
resentment (ree ZENT ment) *n.*: a feeling of displeasure with someone who, one believes, has caused injury or unhappiness
retreated (re TREE ted) *v.*: moved back towards the place it had come from
rivalry (RY vul ree) *n.*: competition [related word]

S

sanctuaries (SANK chew AIR eez) *n.*: a portion of land set aside by the government, where wildlife can live in safety from hunters
sapling (SAP ling) *n.*: young tree
scavenging (SKAH vun jing) *v.*: taking or gathering something useable from among unwanted things
scoffed (SKOFT) *v.*: mocked; ridiculed
semicircular (SEM ee SUR kyuh lur) *adj.*: shaped like half of a circle
shaft *n.*: the long, straight stem of something
shanties (SHAN teez) *n.*: cabins or houses that are roughly built and in a state of disrepair
siege (SEEJ) *n.*: a serious attack, as in illness
singe (SINJ) *v.*: to burn slightly
snare *n.*: a trap

Glossary

soar (SORE) *v.*: fly high into the air
sow (rhymes with now) *n.*: an adult, female pig
sprinted (SPRINT ed) *v.*: raced at full speed for a short distance
spry (SPRY) *adj.*: energetic [related word]
stealthily (STELL thih lee) *adv.*: softly and secretly
stifling (STYF ling) *adj.*: so hot and still as to make it difficult to breathe
stunned (STUND) *v.*: shocked
surpass (sur PASS) *v.*: outdo [related word]
susceptible (suh SEP tih buhl) *adj.*: more likely to be affected by something
suspended (sus SPEND ed) *v.*: temporarily stopped
swig *n.*: a mouthful of liquid
sympathetic (SIM puh THET ik) *adj.*: understanding and supportive

T

technique (tek NEEK) *n.*: method
tenement (TEH nuh munt) *n.*: a run-down and often overcrowded apartment house
tepid (TEP id) *adj.*: lukewarm
thatched *adj.*: having a roof made of straw
thaw *v.*: melt
thicket (THIK it) *n.*: many bushes growing close together
thrashes *v.*: beats against
thrives *v.*: grows and improves
timid (TIH mid) *adj.*: shy and easily frightened
tooling (TOOL ing) *v.*: driving or riding in a vehicle
transactions (tran ZAK shuns) *n.*: buying or selling something [related word]
transport (trans PORT) *v.*: to move; to carry
treacherous (TRECH uh russ) *adj.*: very dangerous
trembling (TREMB ling) *v.*: shaking slightly from fear, cold, or excitement
triumph (TRY umf) *n.*: victory [related word]
trough (TROFF) *n.*: a long, boxlike container used to hold food or water for animals
trudged (TRUJD) *v.*: walked slowly and heavily

U

undulating (UN dyuh LAY ting) *v.*: moving with a wavelike motion
upheaval (up HEE vul) *n.*: a great disturbance

Glossary

V

venture (VEN chur) *v.*: to go carefully into an unknown or dangerous place
vertical (VUR tih kul) *adj.*: going up and down, not from side to side
vicious (VISH uss) *adj.*: harsh and cruel
vigorous (VIG uh russ) *adj.*: active [related word]

W

wallowed (WAH lode) *v.*: rolled about in a clumsy way
wan (WAHN) *adj.*: pale and weak
wedged (WEJD) *v.*: packed in tightly
whiff *n.*: a slight smell
withered (WIH thurd [soft *th* as in *the*]) *adj.*: shriveled [related word]